/FOL

NOT
GUILTY

Other books by George Sullivan
you will enjoy:

Alamo!

In the Line of Fire: Eight Women War Spies

The Day the Women Got the Vote

They Shot the President: Ten True Stories

NOT GUILTY

George Sullivan

Scholastic Inc.

New York   Toronto   London   Auckland   Sydney

Pages 58, 77, 79: Archives of Labor and Urban Affairs, Wayne State University; **pages 32, 53:** Dick Bancroft; **page 2:** Ken Carter; **pages 99, 111:** Library of Congress; **pages 115, 119, 135:** Collection of John F. Marszalek; **pages 51, 84:** George Sullivan; **page 89:** Surratt House Museum; **pages 5, 19, 28, 137:** Wide World.

ISBN 0-590-89749-7

12 11 10 9 8 7 6 5 4 3 2 1   7 8 9/9 0 1 2/0

Printed in the U.S.A.   40

First Scholastic printing, December 1997

Contents

	Introduction	vii
1.	A Fight for Justice	1
2.	Shoot-out at Pine Ridge	31
3.	The Man Who Never Died	56
4.	A Nation's Vengeance	83
5.	Incident at West Point	114
	For Further Reading	139
	Index	143

Introduction

Not long before 4 A.M. on December 9, 1981, in a troubled neighborhood of downtown Philadelphia, police officer Daniel Faulkner was shot to death. He had just stopped a Volkswagen and attempted to arrest its driver, William Cook, for driving the wrong way down a one-way street.

A few months later, Cook's brother, Mumia Abu-Jamal, a well-known radio journalist active in political causes in Philadelphia, was tried and convicted for the police officer's murder and sentenced to die. After a number of postponements, Abu-Jamal's execution was scheduled for August 17, 1995.

During his many years on death row, Abu-Jamal's lawyers campaigned on his behalf. They questioned the fairness of his trial, saying that the police held back evidence that would have helped to demonstrate Abu-Jamal's innocence. They said that the police frightened and bullied witnesses and that the judge was prejudiced against the defense. They called for a new trial for Abu-Jamal.

Abu-Jamal became a symbol for the movement against the death penalty and his case became a cause. Demonstrations on his behalf were held across the country and in Europe. Dozens of celebrities from the art and entertainment worlds joined the "Free Mumia" movement.

The public outcry scored a success. On August 7, 1995, just ten days before he was scheduled to die, Mumia Abu-Jamal was granted an indefinite postponement of his execution.

Mumia Abu-Jamal was fortunate. His thousands of supporters, by putting the spotlight on failures in the criminal justice system and abuses by the Philadelphia police, helped to preserve his life.

Countless others have not been so fortunate. While most Americans trust the nation's criminal justice system and value the dedication of law enforcement officials, they also realize that mistakes can and do occur. Sometimes it is the innocent who are found guilty.

How is it possible for a person to be wrongfully convicted of a crime? Sometimes mistaken testimony by an eyewitness is an important factor. A witness will testify in good faith that he or she saw a crime being committed, but be utterly wrong. Other times, false testimony occurs, that is, a witness deliberately lies.

Miscarriages in justice can also occur when community passions are aroused against the defendant. The news media fan the flames. In the case of Abu-Jamal, who is black, and the victim, a white police officer, racial bias was said to be an issue.

Failure in police work can play a part, too. There are instances of police mishandling evidence, tampering with evidence, or forcing confessions from the accused.

All of these things are shown in this book, which tells of five persons who were wrongly tried and convicted. In one way or another, they were made to suffer because the justice system went awry, and two of them paid with their lives.

NOT
GUILTY

1
A Fight for Justice

That fateful Friday night, a night he would not forget for the rest of his life, began like many others for eighteen-year-old Peter Reilly, a quiet, easygoing high school senior from the tiny town of Falls Village in northwest Connecticut.

In the early evening, Peter and his friend Geoff Madow spent some time at Peter's home with Peter's mother, Barbara Gibbons, while she was having her dinner. Around 7:30, the two boys left for the Canaan Youth Center (called most often the Teen Center) at the Canaan United Methodist Church on West Main Street in North Canaan, about five miles away.

Barbara was watching the news on TV when the boys left. It was the last time Peter would see his mother alive. The date was September 28, 1973.

Peter drove to the Teen Center in his dark blue '68 Chevy Corvette with its white convertible top. Geoff went in his own car. The two didn't go together because Geoff didn't have enough gas to drive Peter home after they left the Teen Center and then drive to his own home.

The two boys stayed at the Teen Center for a couple of hours. Finding a new location for the center was the topic discussed that night.

Peter Reilly's mother, Barbara Gibbons, in a photograph taken in 1973, five months before her death.

Around 9:30, Peter decided to leave. Another of Peter's friends, John Sochocki, asked him for a ride home, so Peter dropped him off at his house. Then Peter went straight home, a journey of five-and-a-half miles.

It was not long before 10:00 P.M. when Peter pulled into the yard and looked for a level spot to park because his emergency brake wasn't working. After he parked the car, he got out to fix a headlight. He jiggled the light a little bit, then got back into the car, shut off the lights, and locked up.

The screen door was open and the front door was ajar. Peter walked in and called out, "Hey, Mom, I'm home." But there was no answer.

Peter figured his mother had probably fallen asleep while reading in bed. She and Peter shared a small bedroom and slept in bunk beds. Peter peered into the bedroom. The top bed, where Barbara always slept, was empty.

Then Peter gasped. There was Barbara, sprawled on the bedroom floor, her throat slashed, her arms outstretched, her legs spread, with blood all over the place. Thinking she might still be alive, Peter yelled to her but she didn't respond.

Peter went to the telephone and called Mickey and Marion Madow, Geoff's parents. Mickey Madow was a volunteer ambulance driver for the area.

"Bring the ambulance!" Peter cried into the telephone. "Something has happened to Mom!"

"Peter, we'll be right there!" Marion said. She and her husband rushed to the ambulance.

Peter also called his doctor, who was not available, and a hospital in nearby Sharon, Connecticut. The hospital sent an ambulance and called the state police, who swarmed to the scene.

An ambulance crew quickly established that Barbara Gibbons was dead. They covered her body with a white blanket.

The Madows assumed that Peter would be asked only routine questions by the police, and then released. They asked the officers to bring Peter to their house when they had finished with him. The officers said they would.

Peter never got to the Madows' house that night. The Connecticut state police took Peter into custody to question him, first at the police barracks in Canaan and the next day in Hartford. Peter talked to the police trustingly, with no friend, lawyer, or other adult present.

He willingly took a lie-detector test. Afterward, he willingly signed a confession and that led to his arrest for the murder of his mother, Barbara Gibbons.

There was not a fragment of physical evidence to link Peter to the crime. There was not a single reliable eyewitness to support his accusers. If Peter had not cooperated so willingly with the police officers whom he trusted, if he had simply exercised his constitutional right to remain silent, there would have been no case against him.

4

This is the story of Peter Reilly, once described as "an easy guy to pick on . . . all alone in the world at the time." It is the story of how police got the exhausted, confused teenager to confess to the brutal murder of his mother and how he was tried and convicted of manslaughter and sentenced to six to sixteen years behind bars.

Accompanied by Marion Madow, Reilly arrives at the court-house in Litchfield, Connecticut, in May 1974 for sentencing. He received a sentence of six to sixteen years.

Almost everyone who knew Peter Reilly believed he could never have done what the police said he had. From the day he was arrested, dozens of friends and neighbors worked to win his freedom, forming a committee to raise the money needed for Peter's release. "I would stake my daughter's life on his innocence," said Jean Beligni, one of the organizers of what came to be called the Peter Reilly Defense Fund.

Mickey and Marion Madow were among the first to be involved in Peter's case. Peter had often visited the Madow home after school. He and Geoff liked to work on their cars in the driveway, and sometimes Peter stayed for dinner and slept overnight. The Madows assured Peter that when his ordeal was over he could have a home with them for as long as he wanted.

Not everyone who sought to support Peter knew him, but those who did liked him and thought well of him. He was a gentle and well-mannered young man, slender, with long hair and a quick smile. He liked to tinker with cars and play his guitar.

Barbara Gibbons, Peter's mother, who said she had been married and divorced, was not thought of so highly. She drank a lot and had a number of boyfriends. Some people resented the fact that she was on welfare, although she appeared to be bright and well educated. She and Peter shared a little four-room house. It had once been a diner.

Peter never seemed bothered by the fact that his last name was different from his mother's. "I don't know who my father was, and I don't think anyone knows," he once said. "She just picked my name out of the air."

Peter and Barbara sometimes bickered and yelled at each other. But they cared for each other and looked out for each other. At Christmas one year, Peter gave Barbara an electric typewriter that he bought with money he had earned playing guitar in a local band. The next spring, she gave him an expensive amplifier.

"My mom never got uptight about anything," Peter once said. "I got used to playing everything by ear. Things work out best that way. They always do."

Just a few minutes after Peter had discovered his mother's body and called the Madows, Geoff Madow's car came flying in to Peter's yard. The two boys went into the house and looked at the body. Geoff turned pale. The boys went into the living room and sat and talked. A couple of minutes later, a police cruiser pulled up, its lights flashing.

Officer Bruce McCafferty of the Connecticut state police jumped out of the car. In the bedroom, Officer McCafferty knelt beside Barbara's body and felt her left wrist for a pulse, but there was none. "Don't move a thing," he told the boys. "Don't touch a thing." Then he went out to his car and radioed the state police barracks. "It looks like I have a possible 125," he said, giving the code number for a homicide.

Before long, the dark night was transformed into a babble of screaming sirens and flashing lights. Mickey Madow reached the scene in his ambulance. More police cars arrived. The assistant medical examiner for the county announced that Barbara Gibbons was DOS — dead on the scene.

Around 10:30, Lieutenant James Shay from the Canaan state police barracks arrived to take charge. Tall and dark-haired, Lieutenant Shay had eight years' experience as a police detective.

Not long after Lieutenant Shay's arrival, Officer McCafferty took Peter into the front seat of his cruiser to have him make a statement for the record. Before McCafferty wrote down what Peter had to say, he gave Peter a paper on which his constitutional rights were printed. In part, they read:

- You have the right to remain silent. If you talk, anything you say can and will be used against you in court.
- You have the right to consult with a lawyer before you are questioned, and you may have him with you during questioning.
- If you wish to answer questions, you have the right to stop answering questions at any time.

Peter put his initials after each of the items, indicating he had read and understood them.

"I, Peter A. Reilly, aged eighteen, of Route Sixty-three, Falls Village, Connecticut, make the following voluntary statement," he began. Then he explained his activities that afternoon and told how, in the early evening, he and Geoff Madow had stayed at Peter's house until 7:20, and then had driven to the Teen Center in North Canaan, where they stayed for a couple of hours. He explained driving home from the Teen Center, dropping off John Sochocki on the way, then arriving home, parking his car, and entering the house to discover his mother's body.

After giving his statement, Peter remained in the cruiser for another three and a half hours. His only break came when he was taken to the kitchen of a neighbor's house where he was stripped and searched. Police found no blood on Peter's clothing or person, or anything else that might tend to link him to the crime.

Sitting in the cruiser after the search, Peter could see the police going in and out of the house and the crowd of spectators that had formed behind the barriers that had been put up.

Around two in the morning, Peter was driven, not to the Madows, as he had been expecting, but to the Connecticut state police barracks not far from the center of Canaan. In a large room with vending machines, which served as a lunchroom, Peter sat and waited until dawn. When Peter asked whether he could lie down and get some sleep, he was told, "Not yet. Wait a few more minutes."

Peter wasn't under arrest. He could have left if he wanted to, but he didn't. He trusted the police.

9

At about six in the morning, Lieutenant Shay, who would be in charge of the investigation and the questioning of Peter, took Peter to a small second-floor interview room. He asked Peter to sign two forms to show that he had been read his rights and that he understood them, and Peter did.

"Am I actually a suspect?" Peter asked.

"Yes, you are a suspect," said Lieutenant Shay. He told Peter that the state would furnish him with an attorney if he could not afford one.

It was around 6:30 in the morning when Lieutenant Shay began questioning Peter, who repeated much of what he had said to Officer McCafferty in making his statement. The questioning continued until about 8:00 A.M.

Afterward, Peter felt that Lieutenant Shay didn't believe that he was telling the truth. He volunteered to take a lie-detector test, feeling that the polygraph, to use its more accepted name, would set matters straight.

"That's a good idea," said Lieutenant Shay. "I'll arrange it for you."

By now, Peter had been awake for more than twenty-four hours. He was shown to a bedroom in the barracks and fell fully clothed into a bed. But Peter kept thinking about all that had happened and the things the police had said to him, and he had trouble falling asleep.

Not long after noon on Saturday, Peter was awakened and driven to police headquarters in Hartford, Connecticut, for lie-detector testing. An officer wrapped a rubber cuff around Peter's upper arm while explaining how a polygraph works.

The machine records a person's pulse rate, breathing, blood pressure, and perspiration. It makes a continuous record of these functions by means of metal pens that draw lines on moving graphs. Changes in the pulse rate, blood pressure, and other functions that occur in response to questions *may* indicate when an individual lies.

But the accuracy of lie-detector testing is often questioned. Judges in most criminal cases do not permit testimony obtained through the use of a lie detector to be introduced as evidence. No one accused of a crime can be required to take a polygraph test. But Peter had volunteered to be tested.

At the state police headquarters in Hartford, Peter was introduced to Sergeant Timothy Kelly, a big man with a gray crew cut, who was built like a football linebacker and wearing civilian clothes. A member of the Connecticut state police for twenty-one years, Sergeant Kelly was chief of the polygraph division.

Peter Reilly was no match for Sergeant Kelly and Lieutenant Shay, his chief questioners. By the time the interrogation began, he had been held in isolation by the police all night and into the next day. He had no lawyer, no one to speak to. The Madows and others had never stopped trying to reach Peter, but the police did not tell him that. He was confused and exhausted.

The interrogation was to last eight hours. Every word was recorded on audiotape.

11

In the early stages, Reilly was questioned by Sergeant Kelly. Then Lieutenant Shay took over and Officer James Mulhern joined in. In the final stages, Kelly and Shay questioned Peter together.

His questioners suggested to Peter Reilly that he may have murdered his mother but was unable to remember doing so because he had a mental problem. This was one exchange:

Shay: Don't be afraid to say, "I did it."

Reilly: Ya, but I'm incriminating myself by saying I did.

Shay: We have, right now, without any word out of your mouth, proof positive —

Reilly: That I did it?

Shay: That you did it.

Reilly: So, okay, then I might as well say I did it.

This was another exchange between Peter and Lieutenant Shay:

Shay: As it stands right now, we know and we feel that we can prove that you were responsible for what happened last night. Just by virtue of the time sequence here, we know you were in that house at a certain time and we know your mother died at a certain time, and the two identify. Okay?

Reilly: What do you mean? Do you think I killed my mother?

Shay: I know you killed your mother.

Reilly: I mean, do you think I kicked and beat on her until she was dead?

Shay: As I said, Pete, I know that your mother died at your hands.

Reilly: In my hands?

Shay: *At* your hands.

Reilly: Because of me.

Shay: Right. Now what we do now is to seek the help you need. We do that by first establishing a trust between you and I. All you got to do is get over the mistrust. You've got to trust someone. I think you ought to trust me.

Reilly: But still, should I really come out and say something that I'm not sure.

Shay: Pete, you're sure.

Reilly: No, I'm not. I mean I'm sure of what you've shown me that I did it, but what I'm not sure of is how I did it.

Shay: Pete, if you don't begin to trust me, you're never going to receive the kind of help that you need, because you've got a problem.

Reilly: Um, could you give me an idea of when it could be arranged for me to see a psychiatrist? I mean I want to go as soon as possible.

Shay: Well, the sooner that you and I sit down here and have our talk, the sooner you'll see a psychiatrist. Now why don't you start and just try to

	trust us enough to put your future in our hands. We won't hurt you.
Reilly:	Okay. I walked into the house. I yelled, "Mom, I'm home." Now maybe she did answer me and maybe she didn't. And, I looked and I know I saw her . . . saw her on the floor. So, should I say I did it now? That I did do it?
Shay:	Peter, you did.
Reilly:	I mean everything's not too clear. Things are still getting clearer. Things are clearing up, you know what I mean?
Shay:	As you trust us more, if you do, things will clear up.

At another point in the interrogation, Sergeant Kelly told Peter Reilly that the police had learned from Reilly's friends that "your mother was always on your back. Constantly."

Sergeant Kelly said, "She'd been bugging you so . . . long that last night you came in the house and [she] started bugging you again, and you snapped. Am I right?"

"I would say you're right," Reilly replied, "but I don't remember doing the things that happened. That's just it. I believe I did it now."

Later that night, Peter Reilly did put his signature on a written statement based upon what he had said during the interrogation. In this so-called confession, Reilly said he killed his mother, slashing her throat with a razor.

14

Once the police had a confession, Peter Reilly was arrested for his mother's murder. He was fingerprinted and handcuffed, then driven to the Litchfield Correctional Center in Litchfield, Connecticut, a red-brick jail that looked out on the village green. They gave him jail clothes and put him in cell 32.

In jail, Peter Reilly explained to a fellow inmate what had happened to him. The inmate was quick to realize that the youth was being accused of a crime he did not commit. To him, Reilly seemed to be the victim of a bum rap. He told Reilly to get a lawyer and to keep his mouth shut, not to say anything to anyone except his lawyer and trusted friends.

On Thursday morning, October 4, six days after the murder, Peter Reilly was brought in handcuffs into Superior Court in the town of Litchfield. Bail was set at $50,000. In order for Reilly to be released, that amount of money would have to be posted with the court as guarantee of Reilly's appearance at trial. Since Reilly and no one he knew had $50,000, Reilly went back to jail.

Meanwhile, friends and neighbors of Reilly's were rallying to his defense. They were convinced that he was innocent, that his rights had been violated, and that he had been railroaded to jail on the strength of a so-called confession.

Raising the bail money became the chief goal of Reilly's supporters. They had weekly fund-raising meetings and held countless tag sales, bake sales, dances, and spaghetti dinners. Weeks passed.

In jail, Peter Reilly spent long hours listening to the radio, watching television, and playing cards. He also read, mostly books about crime and law. His teachers made arrangements to provide him with his schoolbooks and homework assignments.

Many of Reilly's classmates wrote to him, letting him know that they were on his side. Several families, including the Madows, visited him each Saturday, which was visitors' day.

Peter Reilly spent Christmas and New Year's in jail. By that time, the defense committee had managed to raise $6,000. Another $44,000 was needed. More months in jail loomed.

Then fate took a hand. Joan Barthel, a New York freelance writer who had recently purchased a house in Litchfield with her husband, read of Peter Reilly's case in the *Lakeville Journal*, a local newspaper. She arranged to attend a meeting of the Peter Reilly Defense Committee. Little by little, Joan became deeply involved in the case and eventually wrote a book about it.

In mid-December, Joan went to Reilly's pretrial hearing, where Reilly's lie-detector test was presented as evidence. Joan took down in shorthand the questions asked by the police and Reilly's answers. She used big chunks of the testimony in an article she wrote that appeared in a magazine named *New Times* early in 1974.

A woman who read the article telephoned a member of the defense committee and asked, "How much more do you need for bail?"

"Forty-four thousand dollars," she was told.

16

"I'll lend it to you," the woman said. Within a couple of weeks the check had arrived.

After 143 days in the Litchfield County Correctional Center, Peter was free to go home. "Home" was now with the Madows. Within a few days, he was calling Marion and Mickey "Mom" and "Dad."

Peter Reilly's trial began on the first day of March 1974. In what was a serious blow to Reilly's defense, the judge ruled that the tape recordings made during his interrogation and his confession could be used as evidence against him. He made the ruling even though Reilly's lawyer called the confession "involuntary" and "coerced."

Seven weeks later, the jury reached its verdict: Peter Reilly was found guilty of manslaughter in the first degree. (Manslaughter is defined as killing without intent or in an extremely emotional state. Murder is killing with the intent to kill.) Reilly's lawyer had made no effective effort to attack his confession during the trial. No experts were called to explain how innocent persons, especially the young or mentally impaired, can be led to confess to crimes they never committed. No psychiatrists were called to testify about the fact that Reilly, given his age, his isolation, and the shock of events, was particularly vulnerable to the pressures exerted by the police.

When the verdict was announced, Reilly's shoulders slumped and he turned stark white. Some of the women in the packed courtroom began to sob.

Six weeks later, on May 24, 1974, Reilly appeared in court for sentencing. "All that I can say is that I've done nothing," Reilly said, his voice barely audible, while he rubbed tears from his eyes. "I would not be a threat to society. I just want a chance to live a decent life." Peter Reilly was given a sentence of six to sixteen years in prison.

Reilly was released from prison after his supporters raised an additional $10,000 to meet the $60,000 bond. He went to work part-time in a local gas station. His lawyers filed an appeal for a new trial.

There was only a slim chance the appeal would be granted. Reilly's lawyers would have to be able to show that there was "newly discovered evidence," facts or testimony that would tend to produce a different verdict. It seemed very likely that Reilly would be going to prison.

In the fall, Peter Reilly went back to classes at the Housatonic Valley Regional High School, living with the fact that he had been found guilty of a crime that he hadn't committed. The next spring, when he graduated from high school, a local newspaper headline announced: "Convicted Killer Receives Diploma."

Meanwhile, Joan Barthel, whose article in *New Times* magazine had been responsible for raising the money needed for Reilly's bail, had launched a personal campaign to arouse interest in Reilly's case in a number of notables who lived in Litchfield County. Playwright Arthur Miller, novelist

In June 1975, while free on bond following his conviction, Peter Reilly graduated from the Housatonic Valley Regional High School in Falls Village, Connecticut.

William Styron, and director Mike Nichols were among those who responded.

Miller was one of several figures who were to play a key role in helping to overturn the wrongful verdict of Reilly's trial and make clear his innocence. They had been reading of Reilly's case in local newspapers. These men could have shrugged and gone on with their lives. They did not; they chose to get involved. As Donald Connery, author of *Guilty Until Proven Innocent,* a complete account of the Reilly case, put it, "They could have driven by the scene of the accident instead of stopping to help."

Miller, who, at the time, shared with Tennessee Williams the status as one of America's foremost living playwrights, lived in Roxbury, not far from the southern border of Litchfield County. One day he drove up to Canaan to meet Peter Reilly and talk with members of the committee who supported him.

"I am absolutely convinced that Peter Reilly could not have killed his mother," Miller said. "There is not a shred of evidence that says he did."

One of Miller's first moves was to look for an experienced attorney to take on Reilly's case. Money was a problem. One attorney whom Miller spoke with asked for a fee of $100,000. Miller's own law firm eventually put the playwright in touch with T. F. (Thomas Francis) Gilroy Daly of Fairfield, Connecticut. Tall and lean with movie-star good looks, "Roy" Daly had been an assistant district attorney in New York City and had been involved in prosecuting organized crime.

Daly knew he faced an uphill struggle. New trials were rarely granted in the state of Connecticut. He realized that he would have to find new evidence, evidence that had not been presented to the jury in the first trial. And the evidence would have to be so convincing that the jury in the new trial would be most likely to render a different verdict.

But was there any new evidence waiting to be discovered? To answer that question, Daly hired a private detective. His name was Jim Conway. An astute, tough-talking former New York City cop who now lived near Hartford, Conway had followed Peter's case in the newspapers and had come to believe in his claim of innocence. He was to spend several months investigating the case without receiving any fee, and payment for only part of his expenses. He never even received the recognition he deserved.

In their first weeks on the case, Conway and Daly spent much of their time investigating Reilly's movements on the night of the murder. They sought to use the clock to confirm Reilly's innocence.

During Reilly's trial, the prosecution had stated that Reilly had arrived home from the Teen Center between 9:30 and 9:40 P.M. A night supervisor at Sharon Hospital reported that Peter Reilly had called her at 9:40. Officer McCafferty arrived at Reilly's house at 10:02.

But Conway and Daly provided evidence that Reilly had not arrived home until 9:50, or even later. That meant that he wouldn't have had sufficient time to commit the crime, change out of his bloody clothes, hide them, and then make all of the telephone calls that he was known to have made.

Upon leaving the Teen Center, Reilly agreed to drop off John Sochocki, a friend, at his home. Conway spoke to Judy MacNeil, John Sochocki's aunt. She recalled that when John arrived home she had said, "John, you're early."

"Yes," John replied, "Peter drove me back." Mrs. MacNeil looked at the kitchen clock. It was 9:45 P.M.

A police report had established that the driving time from Sochocki's home to Reilly's home was five minutes, twenty-nine seconds. That meant that Reilly had arrived home at about 9:50 P.M.

Conway and Daly benefited from some clever detective work performed by Roger Cohn, a reporter for the *Torrington Register*. Reilly's first telephone call was to the Madows. At the trial, Marion Madow testified that she wasn't sure of the time that she received Peter Reilly's call, but she remembered that she was watching *Kelly's Heroes*, the movie on TV. At the time the telephone rang, some men in the movie were boarding a tank and preparing to cross a river. Cohn called CBS, the network that televised *Kelly's Heroes*, and learned that the scene described by Marion Madow was shown in Canaan at ten seconds past 9:50 P.M.

Reilly had made several other telephone calls that night. He dialed information and got the telephone number of Dr. Charles Bornemann. Jessica Bornemann, Dr. Bornemann's daughter-in-law, answered. (Reilly thought it was Dr. Bornemann's wife.) Mrs. Bornemann explained that her father-in-law was away and gave him the names of other doctors to call. When she came to realize that Reilly was involved in an emergency, she also gave him the name of a local hospital. Mrs. Bornemann said her conversation with Reilly lasted about three minutes. It was about 9:54 P.M., or perhaps a minute or so later, when she hung up, she said.

An article by Cohn supported Reilly's testimony that his mother bought a new wallet on the last day of her life. And sometime between 4 and 5 P.M. she cashed a $100 check at a branch of the Torrington State Bank in Falls Village. She bought a half-gallon bottle of wine at a local liquor store and then visited a supermarket. There, according to the manager, she spent only a few dollars.

Barbara was not known to have made any other purchases that day. But when police searched the house after the murder, they found only sixteen cents. The new wallet was never found nor any of the money that remained from the check that she had cashed.

Reilly's supporters pointed out that the person who committed the crime might have had robbery as a motive. But the police never showed any interest in looking for other suspects. They concentrated on establishing Reilly's guilt.

During Conway's months of detective work, he became aware of several local youths who were well known for their excessive drinking and acts of violence. Conway established that one, possibly two, of these youths, had motives to harm Barbara Gibbons.

While Conway was doing the legwork, Daly was busy lining up experts to testify on Reilly's behalf. One was Dr. Milton Helpern, who had headed the Medical Examiner's Office in New York City for more than twenty years. "He knows more about violent and mysterious deaths than anyone else in the country," *The New York Times* once said of him.

After Dr. Helpern studied the evidence in Reilly's case, and noted the time he had available to perpetrate the murder, and was made aware of the absence of blood on Reilly's clothing or person, he concluded that Peter Reilly could not have committed the crime. He "would appear to be the least likely of suspects," said Dr. Helpern.

Roy Daly also called upon Dr. Herbert Spiegel, an associate clinical professor of psychiatry at the Columbia University College of Physicians and Surgeons. After a psychiatric examination of Peter, Dr. Spiegel, an expert on hypnotism, said that Reilly was a "somewhat immature young man" with a "fragile" personality, and that he was "brainwashed" by the police during the questioning. Dr. Spiegel said the police managed to convince Reilly that because he had no memory of the crime, he must have committed it.

By December 1975, Reilly's case was beginning to attract the attention of influential newspapers and magazines, and of network television. *The New York Times* published a two-part, front-page summary of the case. The article hailed Arthur Miller as the playwright who had "turned detective." It failed, however, to credit Joan Barthel for her role in bringing Miller into the case. *Time* and *Newsweek* were preparing articles. And Mike Wallace was conducting interviews for a *60 Minutes* feature.

Early in 1976, in the same Litchfield courtroom where Peter Reilly was first tried, hearings began on Reilly's petition for a new trial. Roy Daly based his petition on three points:

- A sequence of events that demonstrated that Reilly would not have had enough time to commit the crime without getting blood on himself and his clothes.
- A charge the prosecutor had withheld items of evidence that might tend to prove that Peter was innocent.
- New evidence that eliminated the "alibi defense" of a person "with one, and possibly two motives, to do harm to Barbara Gibbons."

Reilly heard testimony about the sequence of events on the night of the murder. He heard a local minister testify that he had seen Reilly's Corvette pull away from the Teen Center at between 9:40 and 9:45 P.M., "no earlier, no later."

He heard Marion Madow describe the scene from *Kelly's Heroes* that she was watching when Reilly called, and then heard a CBS official testify that the scene was broadcast at exactly 9:50 and 10 seconds.

Dr. Helpern testified that Reilly could not have committed the crime in such close quarters without getting some blood on him. Even if he had thrown away his clothes, said Dr. Helpern, traces of blood would have remained under his fingernails.

Dr. Spiegel testified about Reilly's personality. "Because he had such low self-esteem . . . under conditions of interrogation," Dr. Spiegel said, "he [Reilly] needs support, protection. . . . Without that support and guidance, he can easily be confused." And Dr. Spiegel continued, "he most certainly can easily accept as fact something he knows nothing about."

Judge John A. Speziale's decision was just what Reilly and his supporters were hoping for. He said, ". . . it is readily apparent that a grave injustice has been done, and that upon a new trial it is more than likely that a different result will be reached."

What it meant was that Reilly was to get another chance to prove his innocence. Reilly's lawyer called the judge's decision "a victory for justice."

In the months that followed, Reilly's case took a surprising turn. The original prosecutor suffered a heart attack and died. Dennis Santore, a thirty-one-year-old lawyer from Torrington, Connecticut, was chosen to replace him. Santore said he planned to review all of the files in the case before making a decision to retry Reilly or drop the charges against him.

In going through the files, Santore came upon a key piece of evidence. On the night of the murder, a Canaan auxiliary state trooper and his wife had seen Reilly driving in downtown Canaan at 9:40 P.M., and they told police about it.

Here was evidence that supported the time sequence presented by Reilly's lawyer, Roy Daly, confirming that Reilly would not have had time to commit the crime. Yet the defense was never told of the statement. In other words, vital information that could have been used to establish Reilly's innocence had been kept from Reilly's lawyers for three years.

Immediately, Daly went into court and asked that all charges against Reilly be dismissed.

Dennis Santore, the young and newly appointed state's attorney, could have opposed Daly's request. Lieutenant Shay and other law enforcement officials wanted Peter to be tried again. It would have been easy for Santore to go along with the police. But he did not. He made no objection to Daly's request.

The hearing was held in the Litchfield County courthouse on November 24, 1976, the day before Thanksgiving Day. Superior Court Judge Simon Cohen presided. In his ruling, Judge Cohen declared that the new information made "effective prosecution of the charge extremely doubtful."

Judge Cohen concluded: "I believe, in the best interests of justice, that this case should be dismissed."

Reilly was standing in the same courtroom where he had stood almost three years earlier and heard himself convicted of killing his mother. Now he was being told he was going free. He began to sob softly. "I'm so happy," he repeatedly said. He told his supporters and reporters later at an impromptu gathering, "I just want to go home."

The state of Connecticut later held a special investigation to look into the way the police had handled Reilly's case. In mid-1977, when the results of the investigation were made public, the state police were harshly criticized for their single-minded pursuit of Reilly. The report declared, ". . . after Reilly was charged with the murder, the remainder of the investigation was concerned primarily with the elimination of other suspects."

The report was especially critical of the lie-detector tests that Reilly took, saying they were

After charges against Reilly were dismissed, he and playwright Arthur Miller, who worked diligently on Reilly's behalf, celebrated at a party in Falls Village.

28

used chiefly "to eliminate suspects and prepare a stronger case against Reilly."

"Overzealous" was the word used to describe the police in their efforts to blame Reilly for Barbara Gibbons's murder.

Although Reilly's ordeal had ended, the question remained: Who killed Barbara Gibbons? During the late 1970s, several other persons who had the motivation and opportunity to kill Barbara were linked to the crime. But police lacked sufficient evidence to bring any suspects to trial. The case remained open.

In 1993, on the twentieth anniversary of his mother's death, Reilly spoke to a reporter from the *Hartford Courant*. At the time, he was living in South Windsor, Connecticut, with Mickey and Marion Madow, the first people he had called the night he discovered his mother's body.

"I don't dwell on it," Reilly said of his mother's death and his own ordeal. "I have to move on with my life."

But he did voice concern that there had never been an arrest made in the case. Reilly said, "I felt that if anybody was done a wrong my mother was done a wrong, because she never got justice."

There's a footnote to the Peter Reilly case. In the fall of 1995, almost twenty years after the charges against Reilly had been dismissed, newspaper headlines cried out about a similar case of injustice in Connecticut. Police in Manchester, Connecticut, had arrested Richard Lapointe, a middle-aged brain-damaged man, and charged him with killing his wife's eighty-eight-year-old grandmother in 1987.

Lapointe was tried, convicted, and sentenced to life in prison on the basis of a confession that came about during a ten-hour questioning session. During those ten hours, Lapointe's supporters say, he was denied a lawyer. They also say that he was threatened and prevented from going to the bathroom until he admitted his guilt.

Peter Reilly was one of many individuals who came forward to support Lapointe. Arthur Miller was another. "It's the Peter Reilly case all over again," Miller told *The New York Times*. "I thought we learned something from that: that you cannot base a whole case on a confession, especially in the case of a person of [the] mental capacity of this one."

And Reilly said, "I see the same things happening here that happened to me. Something's wrong with the system, and it has to stop."

2
Shoot-out at Pine Ridge

In 1996, at the age of fifty-one, Leonard Peltier, a burly, soft-spoken Indian of Ojibwa (Chippewa), Cree, Lakota, and French extraction, began serving his twentieth year in the Leavenworth (Kansas) Federal Penitentiary for the killing of two FBI agents.

It's a crime that he and his many thousands of supporters say he did not commit. Moreover, they say his conviction was based on evidence invented by the Federal Bureau of Investigation (FBI).

What makes Peltier's case all the more tragic is that the government recently admitted that it doesn't know for sure who killed the two agents. But a court has ruled that Peltier must remain in prison because government prosecutors say that he participated in the crime.

Leonard Peltier shows surprisingly little bitterness for someone who has been wrongly accused, tried, and convicted. "There's a bad way and a good way of looking at what's happened to me," he says. "Sure, they've taken twenty years of my life. I'll never get that back and nothing they do can ever repay me for that.

"But some good has come out of it," he says. "What the Creator has put me through has helped Indian people. It's kept Indian issues in the forefront for twenty years. It's educated people about what's been happening to Indians on the reservations and also about Indian treaty rights.

"The sacrifice hasn't been for nothing."

The violent and tragic episode that took the lives of the two FBI agents and that was to trans-

Leonard Peltier was sent to prison in 1977, accused of shooting two FBI agents on the Pine Ridge Indian Reservation in South Dakota.

form Leonard Peltier's life and trigger two decades of activism on his behalf took place late on the sun-filled morning of June 26, 1975, on South Dakota's Pine Ridge Indian Reservation near the small village of Oglala.

Located just north of South Dakota's border with Nebraska, the Pine Ridge Reservation's size is its most notable feature. It is enormous. At 4,500 square miles, Pine Ridge is almost as big as two Delawares. Rolling, grassy, flat-topped hills make up much of the terrain.

Pine Ridge is also a deeply troubled place, and has been for more than a century. Over ninety percent of the land is now owned or leased by white ranchers and farmers, or individuals with little Indian blood.

Of the 15,000 or so Indians who have remained on the reservation, about 10,000 of them are Oglala, a branch of the Lakota. There is one library, one bank. There is no industry, no commercial life. The unemployment rate is ten times the national average. The Pine Ridge Indians live in devastating poverty. They are, in fact, the most sickly and socially battered of the nation's Native Americans.

On the June day in question, two FBI agents, Ron Williams and Jack Coler, driving separate cars, headed south, then east across the reservation. The two men were chasing a red pickup truck they believed was being driven by Jimmy Eagle, a boy who had stolen a pair of cowboy boots.

After the pickup truck passed a tall water tank at the small village of Oglala, it turned onto a long dirt road leading to a group of shacks and cabins on a ranch owned by an elderly couple, Harry and Cecilia Jumping Bull. The FBI agents followed.

The pickup truck climbed a bluff, went down the other side, crossed a meadow, and raced up another hill. The agents' cars halted briefly, then took up the chase again.

The red pickup finally stopped. When the driver got out, he was carrying an AR-15, a semiautomatic rifle. The agents stopped, too, one car behind the other. They got out of their cars and took automatic weapons from the trunks. No one knows for sure who fired first, but shots were exchanged.

Leonard Peltier was on the reservation that morning. He was one of a number of members of the American Indian Movement (AIM) who had been called upon by the Jumping Bulls for protection during what had been a long series of clashes with federal agents.

When they heard the bursts of gunfire, Peltier and the other AIM members thought they were being attacked. They started firing back, trying to defend themselves as well as the women, children, and elders who lived in the Jumping Bull camp.

With bullets flying, the driver of the pickup truck got back behind the wheel and drove off. Both agents had been hit by this time.

"We're under fire!" one of the agents reported on his car radio. Then, "I have been hit!" With that, other FBI agents, law enforcement officials from the Bureau of Indian Affairs (BIA), and South Dakota state police and sheriff's deputies swarmed into the area. Soon the Jumping Bulls' ranch was surrounded.

According to the FBI's version of the events, "Coler and Williams were both wounded and defenseless within minutes." But "not satisfied with the terrible injuries they had inflicted, Peltier and two other men walked down the hill toward the ambushed officers. Williams, kneeling and apparently surrendering, was shot in the face through his outstretched shielding hand. He died instantly. Coler, still unconscious, was shot twice in the head at close range." Peltier, the FBI declared, was "the executioner."

Peltier has called the FBI account a "total distortion and outright lies." He remembers the day in much different terms. He says that he awoke to the sound of gunfire. He picked up a rifle and ran in the direction of the shooting. When he reached the scene, he noticed shots coming from the agents' cars as well as from two officers from the BIA who were stranded in the road. He admits that he returned their fire.

"Yes, I shot, I shot," Peltier told an interviewer. "I shot at them. But I believe in my heart it was self-defense.

"I know I shot at them a few times, because when I was running over to one house from another, they were shooting at me. . . .

"These are the same people that were helping terrorize the people. So there was no law for us . . . just because they were law officers, to us didn't mean nothing.

"I never killed the agents," Leonard Peltier told author Peter Matthiessen. "I never even *fired* at them, not directly.

"I just kept firing over their heads, trying to keep them from firing at *us*."

A few minutes after firing the shots, Peltier said, he saw a red pickup truck drive down the hill and stop by the agents' cars. Then he heard three shots. These, apparently, were the shots that killed the agents.

Williams and Coler weren't the only victims of the gun battle, which lasted seven hours. An Indian named Joseph Killsright Stuntz was also shot to death. (The killing of Stuntz was never investigated, much less prosecuted.)

"We lost two guys out there, and we're going to pull out all the stops," said an FBI agent after the smoke had cleared. And he was right. That night, the FBI began airlifting in heavy weapons and high explosives, a search helicopter, armored personnel carriers, and military jeeps. Close to two hundred agents comprised the force. One hundred, dressed in battle gear, were brought in by bus. By dawn the next day, the biggest manhunt in FBI history was underway.

Although more than a dozen Native Americans were targets of the FBI's search, only four men were eventually officially accused of the crime — Jimmy Eagle, Dino Butler, Bob Robideau, and Leonard Peltier. Butler and Robideau were tried in Cedar Rapids, Iowa, during the summer of 1976. The jury ruled self-defense and both men were found not guilty. The charges against Jimmy Eagle were dropped.

The federal government then focused on Peltier, who, earlier, had fled to Canada. Using falsified evidence, the federal government managed to get Canadian officials to give Peltier up, and he was returned to the United States.

Peltier, then thirty-three, was found guilty at the trial in Fargo, North Dakota, and sentenced to two consecutive life terms. In March 1996, following a hearing of the issues in the case, the U.S. Parole Commission denied Peltier an early release from prison. The commission said that he would not be eligible for a rehearing until 2008. By that time, Peltier will have spent thirty-one years in prison. He will be sixty-four.

Leonard Peltier was born on September 12, 1944, in Grand Forks, North Dakota. Most of the year, the Peltier family lived on the Turtle Mountain Indian Reservation, about 150 miles north and west of Grand Forks, close to the Canadian border.

It was harvest time and the Peltier family — grandparents, aunts, uncles, and children — had temporarily migrated to the Red River Valley to work in the potato fields. Potatoes were still being picked by hand and the Indians received three to four cents for each bushel they picked. Later, when Leonard was old enough to go into the fields, he was assigned to work ahead of the pickers, shaking the potatoes loose from the plants, so they could be picked faster.

When Leonard was four, his parents separated. He and his sister, Betty Ann, went to live with their grandparents. "In those days, a lot of Indian grandparents were still raising their grandchildren," Leonard told Peter Matthiessen for *In the Spirit of Crazy Horse*. "It's an old Indian tradition, still being practiced in some Indian nations."

Leonard's grandfather operated a small ranch on reservation land not far from the tiny town of Belcourt, with a few head of cattle and some horses, pigs, and chickens.

In one of his earliest memories, Leonard recalls going with other kids to a big hill about a mile from his home to wait for his grandfather to return from a trip to town with the family's monthly issue of government food and other necessities. Since his grandfather, like most of the other reservation families, had no automobile, he depended on a friend to drive him into town. The friend would drop him off on the main road. As soon as Leonard spotted his grandfather, he would run to him, and then help him carry the groceries home.

When Leonard was about eight years old, the family moved to Butte, Montana, where Leonard's uncles went to work in the copper mines. One day Leonard was confronted by several white youngsters about his age who started yelling, "Hey, you dirty Indian, go home!" Leonard didn't understand what they were saying.

Then the boys started throwing rocks at him. Leonard was hit and hurt, and almost started crying. He picked up a rock about the size of a marble and threw it at one of the boys, and it struck him in the head. The boy started bleeding and screaming. Panicking, Leonard raced home.

Later that day, the boy's mother drove into the Peltiers' yard and hollered for Leonard's parents to come outside. When Leonard's grandmother went out to see what was going on, the woman screamed at her, saying that Leonard had tried to kill her son with a rock. She threatened to have him put in a reformatory. Since Leonard's grandmother spoke Ojibwa and knew only a few words of English, she was unable to answer the woman. That made the woman even angrier.

That night, Leonard's grandfather took Leonard aside and asked him what had happened. Leonard explained how a group of white boys had called him "a dirty Indian" and thrown rocks at him. His grandfather patted Leonard on the head and said, "All those white people are like that."

His grandfather decided that they would all return to the reservation in North Dakota immediately. Most of the family left that night. The others returned the next day. Soon, tragedy touched the Peltier family. Leonard's grandfather caught pneumonia and died.

Leonard's grandfather had always taken care of the family. He cut and hauled firewood, which he sold to families on the reservation. He hunted small game for food, seldom returning from a hunt without at least a rabbit. "After he died, my whole life turned upside down," Leonard says.

Leonard helped out with the chores, hauling wood and water. Like other kids, he carried a slingshot, and used it to occasionally bring down a bird or bag a squirrel, thereby putting meat on the family table.

When his grandmother sought financial assistance for raising Leonard, his sister, and a cousin, the BIA suggested the children might be better off in a foster home. Leonard's grandmother couldn't accept that, but the federal government eventually placed Leonard in the Wahpeton Indian School in Wahpeton, South Dakota. There Leonard was kept under a very tight rein, but he ate regularly and slept in a clean bed every night.

Leonard's mother later secured his release from Wahpeton, and he went to live with her in Grand Forks. There he had an unfortunate brush with the law. Leonard's mother was fearful that their house might soon be without fuel oil, and cold weather was coming. There would be no money to pay for fuel for two weeks, until the family welfare check arrived.

Leonard and a friend, whose family was also without fuel oil, decided to steal diesel fuel from trucks parked on a nearby Army Reserve depot. The diesel fuel could be burned as substitute fuel oil. They parked their car on a road near the base, jumped the fence, made their way for about a mile through deep snow to the trucks, then proceeded to siphon fuel into big cans that they had carried with them.

They made several trips to and from their parked car with the fuel. When they returned to their car on their final trip, cops were waiting for them. Leonard spent two weeks in jail before he was released into his mother's custody.

After that experience, Leonard went to live with his father at the Turtle Mountain Reservation. Most of the people on the reservation lived in terrible poverty, with little or almost nothing to eat. "There was hunger for everybody every day," Leonard once recalled.

One day Leonard attended an Indian meeting and heard an elderly Ojibwa woman plead for help because her children were at home slowly starving to death. "Are there no warriors among our men?" the woman asked. "Why do they not stand up for our starving children?"

The woman's words touched Leonard deeply. He made up his mind that from that day on he would work to help his people.

When he was fourteen, Leonard left home for Oakland, California. There he joined his cousin Bob Robideau and lived with the Robideau family. Leonard later worked as a welder in a Portland, Oregon, shipyard. During the Vietnam War, Leonard enlisted in the Marine Corps but was later discharged for medical reasons.

By the time he was twenty, Leonard Peltier was the part owner of an auto-body shop in Seattle,

Washington. With the second floor of the shop as a headquarters, Peltier provided a wide range of voluntary services to the Indian community. Alcoholics and ex-convicts were among those who sought out Leonard for help.

From Seattle, Peltier drifted south to Arizona, then north to Page, Colorado, where he worked as a carpenter. While there, Peltier first heard about AIM, the American Indian Movement. Founded in Minneapolis, Minnesota, in 1968, AIM is a civil rights organization that seeks to protect the lives and treaty rights of American Indians. Peltier joined AIM and became one of its most active members.

Peltier was living in Milwaukee, Wisconsin, in 1972 when he became deeply involved in an unusual AIM protest. Called the Trail of Broken Treaties March, it took the form of a four-mile-long caravan of cars that left San Francisco in October 1972 with Washington, D.C., as its destination.

The long string of Indian protesters arrived in the nation's capital early in November, just before the 1972 presidential election that year, which pitted Republican Richard Nixon against Democrat George McGovern. AIM and the other organizations involved in the protest had notified government officials of their plans, which included discussion of a twenty-point proposal meant to improve relations between the federal government and the Indians. The proposal essentially asked that all treaties be observed.

No discussion ever took place. When Indian leaders in Washington went to the Bureau of Indian Affairs to discuss promised housing for their chiefs who had made the long journey, they were made to wait and wait. While waiting, they decided to hold a sit-in until they "got results."

Chaos followed. Early in the evening, a government riot squad burst through the door and attacked the Indians in an effort to get them to leave the building. The Indians fought back, forcing the riot squad out. The Indians then barricaded the doors and windows, and occupied the building for a week. The stand-off ended when the government promised to listen to the Indians' claims of injustice (and also agreed to pay $66,000 for the Indians' transportation out of Washington). The twenty points were rejected, however.

After the sit-in at the offices of the BIA, the federal government, embarrassed and angered by what had taken place, took a much harsher attitude toward AIM and its leaders. AIM came to be looked upon as an "extremist organization" by the FBI.

In a memo from the attorney general, the FBI was told to "put AIM leaders under close scrutiny and arrest them on every possible charge. . . ." Three AIM leaders — Dennis Banks, Russell Means, and Leonard Peltier — were made special targets of the FBI.

After AIM's takeover of the BIA building in Washington, Peltier traveled to Milwaukee for a brief stay before moving on to South Dakota and then to Seattle. There he became involved in a struggle for fishing rights for Native Americans of the Puyallup-Nisqually.

Meanwhile, AIM and its leaders were making headlines again. Early in 1973, several Oglala chiefs from the Pine Ridge Reservation asked for AIM's help in the face of injustices they were suffering at the hands of Dick Wilson, who had been elected president of the Pine Ridge Tribal Council — in effect, the tribal chairman — the year before. Using federal funds, Wilson had organized and outfitted a private police force of several hundred supporters who were insulting and taunting the older and more traditional tribal members. The brutal force had come to be known as the "goon squad." In his harassment of tribal elders, Wilson had the all-out support of BIA police and the FBI.

To protest Wilson and the violence he had spawned, AIM leaders organized a caravan of several hundred people that traveled to the village of Wounded Knee, on the Pine Ridge Reservation not far from Oglala. On February 28, 1973, the mass of protesters, which included many women and children, took over the community.

Wounded Knee has special significance for all Native Americans. On December 28, 1890, a band of Lakota Sioux, which had fled into the South Dakota Badlands after the killing of Sitting Bull, surrendered to the U.S. 7th Cavalry near Wounded Knee Creek.

The next day, as the troops were disarming the Indians, someone — an Indian or a soldier, no one is certain who — fired a shot. The troops then opened fire. More than 200 Indian men, women, and children were massacred. Twenty-nine soldiers were killed. Many Indians wounded by gunfire were left on the field and froze to death in a blizzard the next day.

In the 1973 confrontation at Wounded Knee, AIM members and their supporters not only challenged Dick Wilson's leadership but demanded the return of land taken from Native Americans in violation of treaty rights.

The FBI responded with a massive show of force. FBI agents, BIA police, federal marshals, and Dick Wilson's goons, supported by helicopters and equipped with armored personnel carriers, automatic weapons, and according to one source "enough ammunition to wipe out every Indian in the Dakotas," surrounded Wounded Knee, cutting off the few hundred men, women, and children who had occupied the village. Gunfights broke out. Two people were killed and several wounded. The occupation lasted seventy-one days.

After the Wounded Knee siege, the violence between federal forces and the traditional Indians on the Pine Ridge Reservation increased. Shoot-outs, beatings, and killings became almost commonplace. AIM claimed that sixty of its members were killed or "disappeared" following the Wounded Knee occupation.

So it was that in the spring of 1975, Harry and Cecilia Jumping Bull asked AIM leaders to set up a camp on their ranch near Oglala. The Jumping Bulls were fearful of Dick Wilson's goon squad and the violence its members might provoke. Leonard Peltier was one of thirty AIM members to move into the Jumping Bull compound.

On June 26, 1975, when agents Ron Williams and Jack Coler drove their cars onto the Pine Ridge Reservation and into the Jumping Bull camp, they seemed to be ignoring the explosive atmosphere that existed.

After the gunfight, and the deaths of Williams and Coler, Peltier fled to Canada. Many observers agree this was not a wise decision, but ever since the BIA confrontation, Peltier had known he was "marked."

The government had planned to try Peltier along with two other AIM members, Bob Robideau and Dino Butler. When Robideau and Butler were brought to trial in Cedar Rapids, Iowa, in 1976, they were found not guilty and freed.

To get Peltier back from Canada, the federal government turned to Myrtle Poor Bear, a Lakota woman with a long history of mental illness. According to Peltier's supporters, the FBI terrorized Poor Bear into signing two statements in which she claimed to be Peltier's girlfriend and to have seen him actually kill the two FBI agents at the Jumping Bull compound. These statements were completely false. But they gave Canadian authorities a reason to surrender Leonard to the FBI.

Myrtle Poor Bear later testified under oath that she had not been at Oglala at the time of the shooting and that she did not know Peltier, and in fact had never even seen him. She said she had signed the statements because FBI agents had threatened her and her young daughter with harm.

"I stand before you as a proud man," Peltier declared six weeks later when he faced Judge Benson for sentencing. "I feel no guilt! I have done nothing to feel guilty about!"

Judge Benson sentenced Peltier to two life terms in prison, these to run one after the other.

In the years that followed his conviction and sentencing, Peltier's cause attracted enormous support, not only in the United States but in many foreign countries as well. Calls for a new trial and an investigation into the government's conduct of the case have come from fifty-five members of Congress, fifty members of the Canadian parliament, and almost one hundred world religious leaders.

The Leonard Peltier Defense Committee coordinates the work of the more than 175 Peltier support groups in the United States, Canada, Europe, Australia, and New Zealand. The committee publishes a newspaper six times a year, markets Peltier's lithographs, books about Peltier, and an array of T-shirts, bumper stickers, buttons, and other merchandise.

The committee organizes national protests and rallies in support of Peltier and urges Americans to write, fax, or phone the president, attorney general, or U.S. pardon attorney on Peltier's behalf.

"Free Peltier" marches organized by the committee and held in Washington, D.C., rank as the most significant Indian protests in the nation's capital in more than twenty years. More than 750,000 Americans have signed petitions calling for Peltier's freedom. His supporters have collected an estimated twenty-five million signatures worldwide.

Peltier's trial began on March 17, 1977. From the beginning, it was marked by partiality and prejudice.

The transfer of the trial to Fargo, North Dakota, where much anti-Indian feeling prevailed, was one example. Robideau and Butler had been tried in Iowa because there was known to be less bias against Indians there.

Once Peltier's trial got underway, the presiding judge, Paul Benson, ruled that Peltier's lawyers could not plead self-defense on his behalf. That was a heavy blow. Self-defense was the strategy that had been used to win freedom for Robideau and Butler.

Peltier's lawyers were also not permitted to exhibit evidence to demonstrate the climate of fear that existed on the Pine Ridge Reservation in the days before the shoot-out. That fearfulness was a contributing factor in the killings.

Nor were Peltier's lawyers allowed to present the story of Myrtle Poor Bear, and tell how she had been coerced by the FBI into signing false statements. The statements were used to get Canadian authorities to release Peltier to the FBI.

Peltier's lawyers wanted to use Myrtle Poor Bear's testimony as an example of how the FBI had falsely constructed the case against Peltier. But Judge Benson ruled that Myrtle Poor Bear's testimony was "irrelevant."

On April 17, 1977, the jury began its deliberations. It took jury members only about forty-eight hours to reach a verdict. Leonard Peltier was found guilty of two counts of murder in the first degree.

Peltier's case was the subject of a book by Peter Matthiessen titled *In the Spirit of Crazy Horse*. Peltier is the central figure in *Incident at Oglala*, a documentary film produced and narrated by Robert Redford.

Senator Daniel Inouye of Hawaii, former chairman of the Select Committee on Indian Affairs, has long sought to obtain a reduced sentence for Peltier or some other legal means of gaining his release. In a letter written to Attorney General Janet Reno, Inouye and three other senators declared, "As long as the [FBI] misconduct issues in this case are left unresolved, it will be difficult for Native Americans to trust that the U.S. judicial system will accord them with the same justice that it accords to other citizens."

In 1991, in a letter to Senator Inouye, Federal Judge Gerald W. Heaney urged "favorable action" on the request for executive clemency, that is, for forgiveness, for mercy, on Peltier's behalf. Heaney declared that he saw the shoot-out as a consequence of what had taken place at Wounded Knee in 1973, four years before Peltier's trial.

"The United States overreacted at Wounded Knee," said Judge Heaney. "Instead of carefully considering the legitimate grievances of the Native Americans, the response was essentially a military one which culminated in a deadly firefight on June 26, 1975. . . ."

At Peltier's trial, a single .223 caliber shell casing found in the trunk of Agent Coler's car was the chief evidence used against him. The FBI claimed in court that they had linked the shell casing to an AR-15 rifle that Peltier was said to be carrying on the day the agents were shot.

In their efforts to win a new trial for Peltier, his attorneys obtained an FBI report that said laboratory tests proved the AR-15 rifle said to belong to Peltier did not fire *any* of the shell casings found at the scene. The firing pin in Peltier's rifle was different from the firing pin in the rifle linked to the murders. But Peltier's request for a new trial based on this information was turned down.

The government later admitted that it really didn't know who killed the two agents. A federal prosecutor told an appeals court in 1985, "We don't know who killed the agents or what actual participation [Peltier] may have had." But the appeals court declared that Peltier's sentence was justified because he was an "aider and abettor" in the killings.

Greg Red Dog of Haines Falls, New York, campaigns for Peltier's release at FBI headquarters in New York in 1996.

Peltier's supporters say that something is not right here. Peltier was convicted by the jury solely on the claim that he had shot the agents at close range, that he was the "executioner." But now the government says that he was merely one of a number of participants. Still, Peltier has been denied a new trial.

By 1993, Peltier had been denied a new trial three times and been refused any chance of parole until 2008. He and his lawyers then sought another means of winning his release before the end of the century — President Bill Clinton. Late in 1993, they made a formal request for executive clemency, that is, a reduction in Peltier's sentence or an outright granting of his freedom.

In 1994, at an historic meeting with more than 300 tribal leaders, Clinton pledged to "dramatically improve" the federal government's relationship with the nation's more than 500 officially recognized tribes made up of almost 1.9 million Native Americans. Leonard Peltier's supporters said that Clinton could forcibly demonstrate the government's improved attitude by speedily granting Peltier his release.

But it was not an easy decision to make. Clinton realized that in granting clemency to Peltier he ran the risk of angering the FBI. In the summer of 1994, two groups representing some 15,000 active and former FBI agents cautioned the president about any show of pity or mercy toward Peltier.

Most of Peltier's time behind bars has been spent at this federal prison in Leavenworth, Kansas.

Peltier is "playing on sympathy" the group declared in an open letter. "Don't let him get away with it.

"Peltier is simply a vicious thug and murderer, with no respect for human life," the letter said.

Ellen Williams, the mother of Ron Williams, one of the slain FBI agents, told an interviewer that she resented how Peltier's supporters had managed to distort the public's feelings about the case. "It is upsetting that everything is being turned around to make these two boys [her son Ron, twenty-seven, and Jack Coler, twenty-eight] the bad guys while Leonard Peltier is touted as a hero," she said. "It's like my son is being murdered over and over again."

While being held at the Leavenworth Federal Penitentiary, Peltier received hundreds of letters a month from his supporters and others interested in his case, and he kept up a correspondence with many of them.

He sometimes received letters from school children. Occasionally, the Peltier Defense Committee makes arrangements for Leonard Peltier to speak to school classrooms. "I'm amazed at kids today," said Peltier, "and how much they seem to know.

"They ask me about life in prison and what I do during the day. They also want to know what I think of the U.S. government."

Peltier learned to paint in prison, working in oils. His defense committee sold the paintings and lithographs made from them, using the income to spread word of his struggle.

During the two decades of his imprisonment, Peltier's nine children, some of them adopted, grew up. He missed out on the births of five grandchildren. His father died in 1989. Prison officials allowed Peltier to call the dying man in his final days.

Peltier prayed with other Native Americans each Saturday on the prison grounds. "We never pray for ourselves," he told an interviewer. "We pray for everybody.

"I never say, 'God, help me.' It's always 'Help my people, help your people.'"

Despite his wrongful conviction and two decades of imprisonment, Peltier remains confident about the future. "We will be successful," he said. "We will be victorious."

3
The Man Who Never Died

American folklore is rich in fascinating heroes. There's John Smith and Pocahontas; there's Paul Bunyan, Paul Revere, and Davy Crockett — to name only a small handful.

The name Joe Hill must be added to the list.

Joe Hill was a Swedish-born songwriter who had a gift for expressing the spirit of the American worker through his music.

Hill was twenty-three, tall and thin, when he immigrated to America in 1902. After his arrival, he worked at many different jobs.

In 1910, while working on the docks in San Pedro, California, Hill joined a labor union known as the Industrial Workers of the World. The IWW, as it was called, was tough and relentless in dealing with business and industry.

As an IWW member, Joe Hill wrote songs in

support of workers' causes. It wasn't long before many thousands of people were singing Joe Hill's songs. They became a powerful force for organizing workers.

Solidarity, an IWW magazine, hailed Hill's songs for their "lilt and laugh and sparkle" and for their ability to "kindle the fires of revolt in the most crushed spirit and quicken the desire for a fuller life in the most humble slave."

In one of his songs, "What We Want," Joe Hill defined how the IWW appealed to workers of every type:

> *We want the sailor and the tailor and the*
>   *lumberjack,*
> *And all the cooks and laundry girls,*
> *We want the guy that dives for pearls,*
> *The pretty maid that's making curls,*
> *And the baker and the staker and the chimney*
>   *sweep,*
> *We want the man that's slinging hash,*
> *The child who works for little cash,*
> *In One Union grand.*

In 1914, Hill's life took a tragic turn. While campaigning for copper mines in Salt Lake City, Utah, he was arrested on a murder charge, found guilty of the crime, then executed by a firing squad.

During his trial, no direct link was ever made between Joe Hill and the victims of the crime. No motive was ever established. Hill was convicted on the flimsiest of circumstantial evidence.

Born in Sweden, Joe Hill died a martyr's death in 1915 at the age of thirty-six.

Those who supported Joe Hill said that he was framed by Utah copper barons, that the evidence was rigged to produce a guilty verdict. They said that Hill's only crime was being labor's poet and a member of the most militant union of the day.

In the days that followed his execution, a number of daily newspapers said that Hill might become an inspiration to future generations. *The New York Times* predicted "there will grow up a revolutionary group [with] a more or less sincere conviction that he died a hero as well as a martyr."

And in Salt Lake City, the *Deseret News* declared that, in time, Hill would be lifted out of his grave "for glorification."

These predictions came true. Songs were written in Joe Hill's honor, and plays and books were published that told of Hill's knockabout life and tragic death. And to this day, working people in the United States and dozens of other nations gather to sing his songs and pay tribute to his memory. For some, Joe Hill is an American folk hero to this day.

While many people are familiar with the legend of Joe Hill, few know much about his life. Joe Hill's real name was Joel Emanuel Hägglund. He was born in Gavle, Sweden, on October 7, 1879.

Joe's father, a conductor with the railroad, was talented with his hands. He built the family's furniture, a brick oven for baking bread, and installed a system of pipes in the Hägglund home so the family could have running water.

Joe's father even built an organ and learned to play it. In the evening, the Hägglund family often gathered about the organ and sang church songs. As soon as the children were tall enough to reach the keys, they each learned to play.

Music became a vital part of Hill's life. In 1915, when Hill was in prison, in reply to a letter he had received from ten-year-old Katie Phar, who enjoyed singing his songs, he wrote: "I am glad to hear that you are taking lessons and intend to become a musician. I wish I had a chance to take music lessons when I was a kid, but I was not fortunate enough for that because . . . I had no money to spare for music lessons, but by trying hard I picked up what little I know about music without lessons.

"You see, I got music in my blood and it just comes natural for me to play any kind of instrument."

When Joe was eight, his father was seriously injured at work and died. The Hägglunds fell on hard times. Mrs. Hägglund had to take in laundry to buy food and pay bills. The oldest children had to drop out of school and get jobs. Joe went to work in a rope factory, the first in a long series of jobs he held as a young boy.

When Joe turned twenty-three, his mother died. Joe and his twenty-five-year-old brother Paul decided to leave Sweden for the United States. Joe had learned English while working as a crew member on Swedish steamships that operated between Sweden and England. Although he spoke with a heavy accent, he had a good command of the language.

Like many newcomers to the United States, Joe changed his name so that it sounded more American. Joel Hägglund became Joseph Hillstrom, then Joe Hill.

For the first year or so, Joe Hill and his brother remained together in New York, working at whatever jobs they could find. Hill worked for a time in a New York bar cleaning spittoons and "rattling the music box," as he called it — that is, playing the piano. After Paul got a job with a railroad, Joe Hill moved west in search of work.

For most of the next ten years, Hill roamed from one place to another, wherever he could find a job. He stacked wheat in the Dakotas; he worked on Wyoming cattle ranches and dug copper and other metals in the mines of Colorado; he picked fruit in California. He worked in lumber camps and sawmills.

Joe Hill eventually settled down in San Pedro, California, where he toiled as a dock worker. Hill's best friend in California operated a shelter for the hungry and the homeless. There Hill played the piano. As he played, he would often make up new words for well-known songs, mimicking the style of each.

During his time in San Pedro, Hill became aware of the American labor movement, which was going through a period of explosive growth. Violent demonstrations were the order of the day and clashes with police were frequent.

But some gains had been made. The American Federation of Labor (AFL), founded in 1886 and stressing the "bread-and-butter" issues of wages, hours, and safety, had been growing by leaps and bounds. By the early 1900s, its membership had passed the million-member mark.

Joe Hill's involvement in the labor movement had begun in 1910, when he joined a local chapter of the Industrial Workers of the World (IWW). Its members were known as Wobblies.

The IWW had been founded five years earlier to oppose the AFL and its conservative policies. Unlike the AFL, which sought mainly white skilled craftsmen as members, the IWW set out to accept all workers, without regard for skill level, skin color, sex, or national origin.

"One big union" — the OBU — was what the IWW said it wanted. But the organization also wanted to eventually create a classless society in which its workers would control both the economy and government.

Music and singing were important to the IWW. Songs gave the members a common purpose, a sense of unity. Members sang everywhere — in the union halls, on the picket lines, in their homes, and even in jails.

Some IWW songs were "joining songs," meant to recruit new members. Other were "teaching songs," meant to explain an issue or a controversy.

Many IWW songs were collected and reprinted in *The Little Red Song Book*, first published in 1909. The songbook's cover featured a heavily muscled industrial worker and the slogan "To Fan the Flames of Dissent." Designed to fit in one's shirt pocket or the back pocket of one's jeans, the songbook cost ten cents.

In 1911, Joe Hill wrote a song that became an

overnight sensation. It was featured in *The Little Red Song Book* that year.

The song was written to support railroad workers of the Southern Pacific line, who were seeking to organize a union. But the workers were facing defeat because the railroad was hiring substitute workers to replace those who were fired for joining the union. These replacement workers were called "scabs."

Joe Hill's song was a humorous takeoff on a popular song that had been written two years earlier about a railroad worker named Casey Jones. Hill called his song "Casey Jones — the Union Scab."

"Casey Jones — the Union Scab" helped to make Joe Hill famous. Printed on brightly colored cards, the song was sold to raise funds to aid the striking Southern Pacific railroaders. Within a few months after being published, it was being sung by workers in every part of the country.

Joe Hill became one of the leading contributors to *The Little Red Song Book*. The 1913 edition had ten new songs that he had written and three earlier ones. All of the songs concerned the bitter struggle of workers who were sometimes beaten and jailed in their pursuit of IWW goals.

In most cases, Hill wrote his own words to well-known songs, rather than write original music. There were good reasons for this. When a song was needed for a strike, it had to be produced quickly. By using an existing tune, the production time was greatly reduced.

There was another advantage. Even if some of the singers didn't know all the words of a song, they could still hum the tune. No one ever had to feel left out.

During the summer of 1913, the IWW became involved in a stormy campaign to unionize railroad construction workers employed by the Utah Construction Company. The company used every possible means to resist the IWW's efforts.

When the IWW sought to hold a street meeting in Salt Lake City, armed mobsters hired by the construction company moved in, clubbing union leaders with their gun butts. The police stood by, doing nothing. Afterward, the principal Wobbly speaker was charged with the attempted murder of the leader of the armed mob, and several of the Wobblies were jailed for rioting.

Other Wobbly meetings were routed in the same manner that summer. It was as if the business community in Salt Lake City, the police, and the courts had declared war on the Wobblies.

The Wobblies in Utah called for help. Supporters from several states, chiefly Colorado and California, began arriving in Salt Lake City. At the time, Joe Hill was working as a machinist at a copper mine in Park City, Utah. He, too, answered the call and set out for Salt Lake City.

Friends of Hill's introduced him to Swedish families in the area. Hill became particularly close to the Eseliuses. The Eselius family operated a boardinghouse in Murray, about twelve miles from Salt Lake City.

About two hours before midnight on Saturday, January 10, 1914, a tragic incident took place that was to shatter Joe Hill's life and lead eventually to his execution.

John Morrison, who owned a grocery store in Salt Lake City, and his sons, Arling, 17, and Merlin, 14, were getting ready to close the store for the night. Suddenly two armed men wearing red bandannas over their faces entered the store. One of the men rushed toward Mr. Morrison, shouted, "We've got you now!" and opened fire.

While Merlin hid behind shelves at the back of the store, Arling grabbed a revolver and started shooting at the gunman. The gunman fired back. Arling was killed instantly. Mr. Morrison died later that night.

The masked men fled, taking nothing. Merlin slowly emerged from his hiding place. When he saw the bodies of his father and brother, he became hysterical. Still, he managed to call the police.

Revenge was given as a possible motive for the murders. On at least two earlier occasions, Morrison's grocery store had been the target of attempted robberies. But Mr. Morrison had always foiled the attempts by shooting at the robbers, and he had once seriously wounded one of them. It was believed that the same men who had taken part in previous attempts to rob Morrison had returned to settle accounts.

Morrison or his son had wounded one of the men, for a trail of blood was found leading from an alley near the store, through a vacant lot to nearby railroad tracks, along a distance of several blocks. A number of suspects were arrested and questioned in the days that followed. All were released for lack of evidence. A few days after the shooting, Joe Hill was arrested and charged with the crime. But Joe was not released.

Hill's involvement in the murder case came about through a curious sequence of events. Between 11 and 11:30 P.M. on the very night that Morrison and his son were murdered, Hill had shown up at the office of Dr. Frank McHugh, only a few miles from the Morrison grocery store. Hill was seeking treatment for a gunshot wound. A bullet had torn through his left lung and left his body through his back.

"I asked him how he came to be shot," Dr. McHugh was to say later, "and he told me that he and another fellow had quarreled over a girl and he had struck the other man, who had retaliated by shooting him."

Dr. McHugh also said that Hill had told him that he was as much to blame as the other fellow, and that he wanted to keep the affair quiet.

Three days after Hill's visit to his office, Dr. McHugh went to the Salt Lake City police to tell them he had treated Joe Hill for a gunshot wound, and that he may have been involved in the Morrison murder. The governor of Utah had announced a $500 reward for information leading to the arrest and conviction of the killer or killers, and Dr. McHugh believed he might have a chance to collect it. Soon after, police went to Hill's room to arrest him.

Joe Hill was in bed and dozing when four police officers burst into the room. Each had a revolver in his hand. A shot rang out and a bullet grazed Hill's chest and shoulder and smashed into his right hand. The police took Hill to jail and put him behind bars.

Hill was tormented by pain throughout the night. The next morning, he asked to be taken to a hospital to have his wounds treated. Instead, he was placed in solitary confinement and told that he was being charged with the murder of grocer Morrison and his son. "You'd better confess," he was told.

Hill told the police that he didn't know anything about the murders. But they still insisted that he confess.

It soon became obvious that the police were willing to go to almost any length to pin the two murders on Joe Hill. Police officers went to the Eselius boardinghouse and there confronted Betty Eselius Olsen. They told her that Hill had confessed to killing the Morrisons and had given her the murder weapon. "Give us the gun," one officer said. Mrs. Olsen insisted that she knew nothing about any gun.

Hill kept telling the police that he was innocent. When he was questioned about his chest wound, all he would say was that he had been shot in a dispute over a woman. But Hill refused to name the woman. He said that if he did so her reputation would be ruined. Nor would he give police the name of the man who shot him. "Where or why I got that wound is nobody's business but my own," Hill said.

By this time, a campaign to establish Hill's guilt was well underway. The police made no secret of the fact that they regarded Joe Hill as their prime suspect. "The police now believe that the circumstantial evidence all points to the guilt of Joe Hill . . ." the police announced to the press soon after Hill's arrest.

It's easy to understand why the police were eager to blame Joe Hill for the murders of John and Arling Morrison. A crime wave had engulfed Salt Lake City, and the police were helpless in its wake. The *Deseret News* called the killing of the Morrisons the "culmination of a series of bold crimes," and noted that local citizens were growing apprehensive over the failure of police to make any arrests. Hill was seen by the police as the solution to their problem.

The press seemed just as eager to convict Joe Hill. The *Deseret News* portrayed Hill as if he were a longtime criminal. Following a courtroom hearing, the newspaper said that Hill "wore a hardened look, betraying no nervousness, his features showing no emotion; and he seemed callous to what was going on."

The newspaper also presented a distorted picture of Hill's past, saying that he had once been arrested in Los Angeles as "a car robbery suspect." Hill protested. He said that he had been arrested only once in his life, and that was during a dock workers' strike in San Pedro.

The *Deseret News* also offered a series of articles on dangers facing Salt Lake City from the IWW and its doctrines of "destruction." The newspaper attacked Joe Hill as a militant member of the organization, a troublemaker, an agitator. Hill was condemned for writing "inflammatory" and "sacrilegious" songs.

Once Hill's trial began, the prosecution, in attempting to link him with the murders, made much of the gun wound that Hill had suffered. Doctors testified that the bullet that wounded Joe Hill passed all the way through his body. Thus, the bullet itself should have been found in the store. Although police searched the store several times, no bullet was ever recovered. Nor was any blood other than Morrison's found in the store.

As for the traces of blood found outside the store and thought to be the blood of one of the robbers, the defense questioned whether it was really human blood. It might be the blood of a dog or some other wounded animal, the defense said. The prosecution declared that "expert testimony would be used to show that the blood was that of a human being." But no "expert testimony" was ever introduced.

The prosecution also made an issue of a red bandanna that police had found in Hill's room. Merlin Morrison testified that both of the gunmen had worn red bandannas over their faces.

But Mrs. Betty Eselius Olsen, testifying for the defense, said that the red bandanna that police had found belonged to her. She had given it to Hill, she said, on the Sunday morning after he had been shot.

In an effort to establish that Joe Hill was one of the men who had entered Morrison's grocery store on the night of the murders, the prosecution attorney called upon fourteen-year-old Merlin Morrison, the only witness to the crime, to identify Hill.

But Merlin could not make a positive identification. All he could say was that Hill's height was "about the same" as that of the gunman who shot his father and brother.

The prosecution also called upon Mrs. Phoebe Seeley to testify. Mrs. Seeley and her husband happened to be walking near the Morrison store before the murders took place. They passed two men, one tall, the other short. Mrs. Seeley said that she and the taller man looked directly at one another.

But Mrs. Seeley was unable to say positively that the man she saw at the crime scene was Joe Hill. Her testimony was loaded with such phrases as "about the same," "appears to be the same," and "seemed to be the same."

In their closing argument, Joe Hill's lawyers stressed his lack of motive, calling it "the weak point" in the prosecution's case. Robbery was not the motive, one of Hill's lawyers pointed out. "No attempt was made to rob the store, no word of robbery was spoken. . . . No one was asked to throw up his hands," Hill's lawyer said. "The murderers merely exclaimed to Morrison, 'We've got you now!' — and then began shooting."

Hill's lawyer pointed out that there was no evidence that Hill even knew Morrison. "Their lives never crossed," he said. "Surely he had no reason for killing him."

Since the prosecution had no facts that could be used to establish Hill's guilt, they had to use other tactics in attempting to sway the jury. They began by attacking Hill's character. One of the prosecuting attorneys denounced Hill as a brute, a fiend, and a parasite on society. He described Joe Hill as "some bloodless thing . . . some thing in which runs the acid of hate."

The prosecution made much of Hill's refusal to take the witness stand and explain how he had been wounded. "Joseph Hillstrom," said one of the prosecuting attorneys, pointing at him, "if you were an innocent man, you would have told us how you received that wound. Why in God's name did you not tell, so your name could have been cleared from the stain upon it?"

Joe Hill also came under attack because he was an active member of the IWW. While there was no direct reference to the IWW itself, the jurors understood that the organization was being referred to when one of the prosecutors urged that Hill be found guilty "so that you and your sons and all upright men shall walk the earth free from the danger of those parasites on society who murder and rob rather than make an honest living."

In their efforts to establish Hill's guilt, the prosecution had no direct evidence, only circumstantial evidence. This is evidence based on events related to the crime from which the jury might infer that Hill might have committed the crime.

A key element in Hill's trial was how Judge M. L. Ritchie intended to explain circumstantial evidence to the jury. The lawyers defending Hill hoped that the judge would compare such evidence to a long chain. Each link in the chain depended on another. If any link were to be broken — if any piece of evidence could not be proven beyond a reasonable doubt — the chain would be destroyed, and Hill would have to be declared not guilty.

The prosecution, on the other hand, hoped Judge Ritchie would say that circumstantial evidence was more in the nature of a heavy cable. While one or more strands of the cable might be broken, the cable itself would still be strong enough to lift a heavy load, that is, support a conviction.

Some two decades earlier, in 1894, the Supreme Court had ruled that in cases involving circumstantial evidence "the chain of circumstances must be complete and unbroken." And courts in Utah had always followed this judgment. Not Judge Ritchie. His instructions to the jury supported the prosecution's point of view, unfortunately for Joe Hill. Judge Ritchie told the jurors that "one weak strand or thread" would not necessarily cause the case to collapse.

Hill's case was given to the jury late on the afternoon of June 26, 1915. The next morning, the jurors were ready with a verdict. They found Joe Hill guilty of murder in the first degree.

Hill took the news calmly, coolly. The *Deseret News* noted that he heard the verdict "without the flutter of an eye," adding, "there was not even a change of color in his cheeks."

As he was leaving the courtroom, Hill turned to a newspaper reporter and declared that he was innocent of the killing and that "he would prove it before he got through."

In Utah at the time, a person convicted of first degree murder faced the death penalty. Judge Ritchie made no exception in Hill's case. Hill was, however, permitted to choose the manner in which the sentence would be carried out — by hanging or shooting. "I'll take shooting," Hill told Judge Ritchie. "I'm used to that. I've been shot at a few times in the past, and I guess I can stand it again."

Judge Ritchie passed sentence on July 8, telling Joe Hill "that on September 4, within the exterior walls of the state prison, between the hours of sunrise and sunset, you [will] be shot until you are dead by the sheriff of Salt Lake County."

Hill's sentencing triggered a storm of protest. Cards, letters, telegrams, and petitions from every part of the country began to pour into the offices of district attorneys throughout the state of Utah, demanding either a new trial for Hill or that he be pardoned. The governor's office was also flooded with protest mail. A letter from E. E. Hahn of Yale, Oklahoma, was typical. Hahn said that he had been watching Hill's trial and "can see no justice in murdering a man on circumstantial evidence."

The protests came not only from IWW members and organizations. They came from hundreds of workers in Tacoma, Washington; the Women's Christian Temperance Union of California; the Italian Socialist Federation of Detroit; the granite workers of Barre, Vermont; the Russian Red Cross Society of Chicago; and countless other individuals and organizations.

The IWW distributed thousands of leaflets to members, calling for protests on Joe Hill's behalf. And the organization issued a special Joe Hill edition of *The Little Red Song Book.*

Members of a chapter of the United Mine Workers in Hillsboro, Illinois, wrote to President Woodrow Wilson, calling for a "new and fair trial" for Joe Hill. What one writer called "perhaps the most famous protest movement in American labor history" became international in scope when IWW members in London passed a resolution "joining with their fellow workers of America in demanding the unconditional release of Joe Hill."

Meanwhile, Hill's lawyers were busy. They had been successful in getting the execution postponed, not once but twice. However, Judge Ritchie turned down their request for a new trial. And an appeal to the Supreme Court to have the trial verdict reversed was also rejected.

Despite these setbacks, there was no letup in the

campaign to save Hill. The IWW vowed to "fight to the very end." As the letters and telegrams continued to flood in, the Salt Lake City *Telegram* noted that "no murder case ever tried in the courts in Utah has attracted wider interest than that of Hillstrom's. . . ."

As the protests kept growing in number and intensity, authorities in Salt Lake City, fearing violence, got jittery. They beefed up the local police force and hired private security guards to protect banks, hotels, and the city's Mormon temple grounds. The homes of the governor and the attorneys who had prosecuted Hill were guarded day and night.

There were even rumors that an army of IWW members might attack the state prison and attempt to free Hill. As a result, prison officials doubled the number of guards. They also borrowed machine guns from the state militia and set them up at the prison entrances.

As for Hill himself, they placed him under heavy guard in solitary confinement. No one was permitted to see him.

By this time, hundreds of Swedes and Swedish organizations in the United States had become aware of Hill's plight. Since Joe Hill was still a Swedish citizen, they called upon W. A. F. Ekengren, the Swedish minister to the United States, and asked him to attempt to delay Hill's execution.

But Ekengren's efforts on Hill's behalf were frustrated by Utah's governor, who declared that "Hillstrom had a fair trial" and was properly found guilty. He accused the ambassador of being "unfamiliar with the record or the real facts in the case."

At the same time the Swedish ambassador was mounting appeals on Hill's behalf, preparations were moving ahead for his execution. It was now scheduled for October 1, 1915.

Just forty-eight hours before Hill was to be shot to death, President Wilson telegraphed Utah's governor, asking him to postpone the execution. He did — but only until the next meeting of the Board of Pardons, which was set for October 16.

In his reply to the president, the governor insisted that Hill had had a fair trial and remarked that he was acting "upon your request and your request only." The governor told reporters "that it was the first time . . . that he heard of the President of the United States interfering in a state case."

At the meeting of the Board of Pardons, Joe Hill was again sentenced to be shot, this time on November 19, 1915, at the state prison in Sugarhouse.

Although the legal battle to save Hill's life continued, it seemed hopeless. Joe Hill himself realized this. In a telegram to Ekengren sent a week before the execution date, Hill asked the Swedish ambassador not to spend any more money on him. "The case is closed," Hill said. "Now my friends know I'm innocent and I don't care what the rest think."

The day before the execution was to take place,

Staging The Murder of Joe Hill at Salt Lake

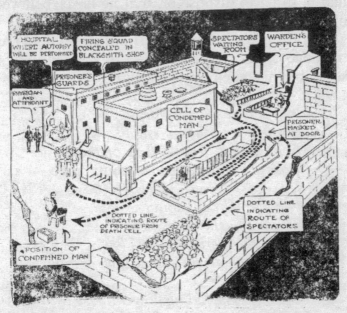

Not long before his execution, the Cleveland Press *published this sketch of Utah State Prison, showing how Hill was to be put to death.*

Joe Hill spent much of his time with a reporter from the Salt Lake City *Herald-Republican*. The reporter found Joe Hill to be composed and confident. "There was an absolute lack of nervousness," the reporter wrote. "His hands, protruding through the bars, were reposeful . . . his eyes were clear, bright, and intelligent . . . his natural sense of humor did not leave him. . . ."

At the end of the interview, the reporter asked Hill how he planned to dispose of his personal belongings, his "little trinkets." Hill replied that he had nothing to dispose of, that he never believed in keepsakes.

According to the reporter, Hill then sat down on the edge of his cot and wrote out the lyrics for a song that he called "My Last Will":

My will is easy to decide,
For there is nothing to divide.
My kin don't need to fuss or moan —
"Moss does not cling to a rolling stone."

My body? Ah! If I could choose,
I would to ashes it reduce,
And let the merry breezes blow
My dust to where some flowers grow.

Perhaps some fading flower then
Would come to life and bloom again.
This is my last and final will.
Good luck to all of you.

Joe Hill

On the morning of November 19, 1915, Joe Hill was taken from his prison cell under heavy guard, brought into the prison yard, and strapped into a chair before a squad of five men armed with rifles. Four of the rifles were loaded with live bullets, one had blanks.

"Aim!" the sheriff ordered.

"Yes, aim!" Hill cried out. "Let her go. Fire!"

78

Joe Hill's funeral procession in Chicago attracted many thousands of mourners.

"Fire!" the sheriff ordered.

The sharp crack of rifle fire pierced the morning stillness. Four bullets ripped into the paper target that had been placed over Joe Hill's heart. At 7:42 A.M., Hill was pronounced dead.

Hill's body was first taken to a funeral home in Salt Lake City where it was viewed by thousands of his supporters. Funeral services were held at the West Side Auditorium in Chicago. More than three thousand mourners crowded into the building. Almost ten times that number stood in streets outside.

On a banner above Joe Hill's coffin and in the program containing the words to the songs that

79

were sung during the services appeared this inscription: "In Memoriam, Joe Hill. We never forget. Murdered by the authorities of the state of Utah, Nov. 19, 1915."

After the services, Hill's body was taken by train to a Chicago cemetery to be cremated. An army of mourners that stretched for more than a mile accompanied the body to the train station.

On November 19, 1916, the first anniversary of Hill's execution, delegates to an annual convention of the IWW met at the West Side Auditorium in Chicago, where the funeral services for Hill had been held. They received small envelopes containing Hill's ashes and were instructed to distribute the ashes when they returned to their home states.

"By this means," said an article in the *Industrial Worker*, "the last will of Joe Hill will be carried out. The breezes will carry this dust to where some flowers grow, and they, revived and nourished, will bloom all the fairer. . . ."

In the years that followed, the IWW all but faded away. During World War I, IWW members refused to sign "no strike" pledges and were branded as being anti-American as a result. Membership nosedived after the war ended in 1918.

While the IWW dwindled in importance, the legend of Joe Hill kept gathering strength. In 1925, Alfred Hayes took a song by Earl Robinson and wrote words to it in Hill's honor:

> *I dreamed I saw Joe Hill last night.*
> *Alive as you and me.*

Says I, "But Joe, you're ten years dead."
"I never died," says he.
"I never died," says he.

"I Dreamed I Saw Joe Hill" carried his name to every corner of the globe.

In 1931, American playwright Barrie Stavis heard protesters in New York singing one of Joe Hill's songs. He became intensely interested in Hill as a result and began collecting information about him. Stavis later began a long period of serious research into Hill's life. Stavis's play *The Man Who Never Died* was published in 1954.

The play has since been translated into more than a dozen languages and has been presented on the stage, on television, and in concert performances. It has even been performed as an opera.

When first published, the play "apparently hit a live nerve," Stavis once recalled, and it "put into motion widespread interest in Joe Hill."

That interest has continued to recent times. A one-hour CD of songs, poems, and narrations by and about Joe Hill was released in 1991. The late Paul Robeson, a noted African-American actor and singer, sings one of the songs. Pete Seeger and other folk artists sing others.

In 1995, to commemorate the eightieth anniversary of his death, the Swedish government issued a stamp in Hill's honor. The same year, the Mine, Mill, and Smelter Workers of Canada presented an updated version of *The Man Who Never Died*. And in Sheffield, England, a theater group known as Rebels United staged *The Dream of Joe Hill*, a play by Liverpool writer John Fay.

"Joe Hill truly was one of the great men of this century . . ." said folk singer Pete Seeger in an introduction he wrote for *The Man Who Never Died*.

Said Seeger: He showed "that it was possible to be humorous and serious at the same time — to be musical and also totally committed to the cause of bringing working people of the world together. . . . He was brave, generous, lighthearted . . . thoughtful towards others, and always militant.

"Though he died before I was born, I feel that his spirit is very much alive with all of us right now."

4

A Nation's Vengeance

In the hours before daybreak on February 12, 1990, Abraham Lincoln's birthday, Army Captain David Osborne was asleep in his quarters at Fort Lesley J. McNair in southwest Washington, D.C. Suddenly, Osborne was awakened by the gut-wrenching sounds of moaning and weeping.

"It was a female voice," he recalled, "and it was crying out, 'Oh, help me, help me!'

"It was coming out of the basement," Osborne said.

Osborne jumped out of bed and raced to the door leading to the basement of Quarters 20, where he lived. When he threw open the door, there was nothing there. He listened intently but the only sound he heard was the whistling wind.

Osborne knew what some of his fellow officers would say when he told them of the experience.

The trial of the conspirators was held on the third floor of this building, now part of Fort Lesley J. McNair in Washington, D.C. The ghost of Mary Surratt is said to haunt the building.

The voice, of course, was that of the ghost of Mary Surratt, hanged at what is now Fort McNair on July 7, 1865.

A smallish, plain-looking forty-two-year-old widow, gentle and deeply religious, Mary Surratt was convicted by a military court of helping John

Wilkes Booth assassinate Abraham Lincoln. She was the first woman in history to be executed by the federal government.

In the weeks following the murder of the sixteenth president, the national was engulfed in a great wave of hate, fear, and terror as soldiers and police arrested and jailed scores of people who were branded as "conspirators" in the assassination plot. Seven others besides Mary Surratt were tried and convicted. Three others paid with their lives.

Mary Surratt said she knew of no conspiracy. She never even knew that Booth had taken it into his head to murder the president. It was a plan of his own design, concocted on short notice.

Ever since Mary Surratt's death, there have been mysterious happenings at Fort McNair. Unusual lights have been seen flashing in the vicinity of Quarters 20 during the night. Furniture moves about. Pictures become tilted on the walls.

"There's a presence here," says Walter Knauss, a retired army sergeant-major who served for ten years at the fort. "I've talked to too many people who have seen her or heard her weeping and wailing."

Knauss's daughter Jennifer and other soldiers' children have told of sighting a veiled "lady in black." And Knauss himself tells of a pane of glass in the room where Mary Surratt was held that frosts over mysteriously. "And when you replace the pane," says Knauss, "the new pane frosts over."

More than a few people believe that the ghost of Mary E. Surratt will not rest until her name is cleared.

Years before she had the great misfortune to cross paths with John Wilkes Booth, Mary Surratt operated a farm and tavern in southern Maryland. The government had made her husband, John Surratt, a postmaster, and the tavern a polling place, calling the crossroads community Surrattsville. The couple had three children, Isaac, Anna, and John, Jr.

After the sudden death of her husband in the summer of 1862, Surratt found the Maryland farm and tavern difficult to run, even though John, Jr., dropped out of St. Charles College near Ellicott's Mills, Maryland, to lend a hand. The fact that the Civil War was raging at the time did not help matters. In November 1864, Mary Surratt decided to lease the tavern to an ex-policeman named John Lloyd.

Lloyd was not the best possible tenant. He drank too much and did not have a good reputation. But Surratt had little choice; she needed the money the lease would provide.

She moved into a three-story house with a low-ceilinged attic on H Street in Washington that her husband had acquired ten years before. John, twenty years old at the time, tall, blond, and intelligent, and the attractive seventeen-year-old Anna went with her. Isaac had left home and become a Confederate cavalryman. Mary Surratt turned the house into a comfortable boardinghouse, providing rooms and regular meals. To attract boarders, she advertised in two Washington papers, the *Star* and the *National Intelligencer*.

There can be no doubt that in the struggle between the states Mary Surratt supported the Confederate cause. She was convinced the North had been wrong to invade the South.

John Surratt also supported the South but much more actively than his mother. John worked as a clerk for the Adams Express Company in Washington and in his spare time served as a Confederate courier and spy, passing messages between Washington, D.C.; Richmond, Virginia; and Canada.

When John was at the Surratt boardinghouse on H Street, he shared a third-floor bedroom with Louis J. Weichmann, who had been a classmate of his at St. Charles. Weichmann had flunked out, taught school for a time, then took a job as a clerk in the office of the Commissary General of Prisoners, a branch of the War Department. Weichmann was fat and soft, a large young man with a sneaky manner.

It is likely that John Surratt, Jr., first met John Wilkes Booth in 1861 when he was introduced to the actor by a boyhood friend. The two met several times after that. On each occasion, Booth sought to sound out Surratt and his feelings about the war and the president. Finally, late in 1864, after he had become aware that John was a Confederate spy, Booth revealed to him a bold plan he had devised to kidnap President Lincoln and hold him hostage in Richmond, the capital of the Confederacy.

After the kidnapping, Booth planned to exchange the president for an army of Confederate prisoners. It was no secret that the South was running low on manpower. The returned prisoners would be used to bolster the Confederate forces.

Booth stressed that they were not going to "kidnap" the president. Kidnapping was a crime. They were going to "capture" him. As Commander in Chief of the Union armies, Lincoln was a military man, Booth explained, and as such ran the risk of being captured.

The more that John Surratt thought about the plan, the more it appealed to him, and he decided to join in. One of his first moves was to invite two others into the conspiracy. One was brawny George Atzerodt, who lived in (and was nicknamed) Port Tobacco, on the Maryland side of the Potomac River, south of Washington, D.C. Atzerodt was a carriage painter who sometimes earned money as a ferryman for Confederate spies.

Surratt also persuaded twenty-three-year-old David Herold, an unemployed drugstore clerk, to join the group. Herold lived with his widowed mother and seven sisters in Washington.

Booth himself enticed several others to join the group, including Lewis Powell, twenty, who had deserted the Confederate Army after the Battle of Gettysburg and now called himself Lewis Paine. Paine was tall and muscular, the team's "young giant."

Mary Surratt paid with her life after being convicted of conspiracy in the assassination of President Abraham Lincoln.

Occasionally, Booth and his band of schemers would meet at Mary Surratt's boardinghouse. They would assemble in one of the upstairs rooms where they would speak in hushed tones while inspecting their arsenal of revolvers and knives.

Mary Surratt came to know a number of the men. She liked Booth, who always played the role of a courtly Southern gentleman whenever she met him. One she didn't like was George Atzerodt, who had a fierce look and a serious drinking problem.

The conspirators sometimes attracted the attention of Louis Weichmann, Mary Surratt's fat and nosy boarder. Once he became aware of the strange get-togethers at the boardinghouse, Weichmann kept his ears open. When he added up all that he had heard and overheard, he came to realize that these people were scheming to kidnap the president.

Weichmann couldn't wait to tell others in his office of his suspicions. The talk eventually reached the ears of his superiors and Weichmann was called upon to make a full report, which he did. It is likely the report ended in a file drawer, for nothing was ever heard of it.

In mid-March, Booth announced a dramatic plan to the conspirators. During the performance of a play at Ford's Theatre, they would seize Lincoln, tie him up, and lower his trussed body from his box to the stage, and into a waiting carriage. Then Booth and his plotters would whisk the president away across the Navy Yard Bridge and into Maryland.

Booth's men raised their voices in opposition to the plan, saying it was foolish and much too dangerous, that it would never work. Booth abandoned the idea.

But he kept thinking. Not long after, Booth learned that the president planned to make an afternoon visit to a Soldiers' Home out on Seventh Street in Washington. Booth proposed that they lie in wait for the president's carriage on a lonely stretch of road, overcome the guards, and then make off with him.

On a cold gray day, the conspirators put their plan into action. When Booth and Surratt stopped the carriage and looked inside, the president was not there. The conspirators had failed.

There was much anger and cursing after that, and the conspirators broke up. Surratt and Paine hurried back to the boardinghouse on H Street. Sam Arnold and Michael O'Laughlin, the two old friends of Booth's whom he had recruited to help in the kidnapping, journeyed to Baltimore.

Booth and his conspirators had had enough of kidnap plots. They would not attempt another.

So far, Mary Surratt had committed no crime for which she could be charged. Yes, her house had been used by men who had plotted to kidnap the president, and several of them visited frequently. She saw them, she talked to them. But no evidence exists that she was at all involved in the conspiracy.

Mary Surratt's trouble began soon after the

failed kidnap attempt. Booth had acquired two rifles, several pistols, ammunition, and knives that were to have been used in the kidnapping. After the plan backfired, it was decided to store the rifles — short-barreled weapons known as carbines — at the Surratt Tavern in Surrattsville.

John Surratt, Jr., drove out to Surrattsville and asked John Lloyd, who had leased the tavern from his mother, to hide the two carbines for him. Lloyd said he wanted nothing to do with the guns.

Surratt insisted. He said he knew of an excellent hiding place. He led Lloyd to a tiny, unfinished attic over the kitchen from which he was able to thrust the rifles between the heavy beams supporting an adjacent bedroom.

"We'll be back to pick them up in a few days," Surratt said.

But Surratt did not return. The rifles remained in their hiding place until the night of Lincoln's murder and were to serve as important evidence in the case against Mary Surratt.

With no plans to put into action, the conspirators split up. Booth and Paine went to New York. John Surratt traveled to Richmond and later left by train for Canada, a long, slow journey. His mission had to do with an attempt to win freedom for Confederate prisoners held in New York State. It is believed that John was in Elmira, New York, on the night that Booth assassinated Lincoln.

Meanwhile, after four years of war, the Confederacy was breathing its last. On April 2, 1865,

Union forces captured Richmond and the Confederate leaders fled the city. About one week later, General Lee surrendered to General Grant. Although the people of Washington were weary from celebrating the fall of Richmond, with Lee's surrender they started celebrating all over again.

Newspaper accounts of what was happening sickened Booth. "My God, I no longer have a country!" he is believed to have said.

Booth now realized there was no longer any reason to make Lincoln his prisoner. He began to think about assassinating him. It would be a way of avenging all the wrongs Booth believed the South had suffered because of the president. And the great blow, he apparently believed, would be a way of assuring lasting fame for himself.

On the evening of April 11, the official celebration of Lee's surrender was scheduled to take place. Mary Surratt was in a grim mood. It wasn't merely because of the defeat of the Confederacy. She was being pressed for payment by a man to whom her husband had owed money.

To solve the problem, she made up her mind to collect $479 that a Mr. John Nothey owed her for some land he had bought from her husband many years before. With the money from Nothey, she could pay the annoying creditor.

That morning, Mary Surratt set out for Surrattsville by buggy to see Nothey. Her son John usually drove her, but since he was away, Louis Weichmann served as her driver.

On the way, they passed a buggy going in the opposite direction. It was driven by John Lloyd, to whom Mary Surratt had leased the tavern. Lloyd pulled to a stop and so did Weichmann. Then Mary Surratt and Lloyd chatted. Weichmann tried to listen but he was unable to hear what was said.

Mary Surratt and Weichmann arrived at the Surratt Tavern around noontime. Later in the day, she met with Nothey but nothing was settled, and she and Weichmann returned to Washington.

Mary Surratt planned a second trip to Surrattsville, again to see Nothey in an effort to collect the money due her. She asked Weichmann to rent a horse and buggy to take her. The date was April 14, 1865, a fateful day.

It was on the morning of April 14 that Booth learned that President Lincoln and his wife had made plans to attend Ford's Theatre that evening for a benefit performance of *Our American Cousin*. The news electrified the actor. He had suddenly been presented with what he believed was the perfect opportunity to strike.

Booth knew every inch of Ford's Theatre from top to bottom. He knew the box in which the president would be seated. He knew that Lincoln's favorite rocking chair would be placed in the box and that Mrs. Lincoln would be seated to the president's right. He also knew that the lock to the box's outer door was broken. The door could not be locked; it could be opened with a gentle shove.

Booth made preparations hastily. He assembled

those members of his band of conspirators who were still in Washington — Herold, Paine, and Atzerodt. He had expanded his plans to include not only the murder of the president but the assassination of other government leaders as well. He assigned Atzerodt to kill Vice President Andrew Johnson, while Paine would do away with Secretary of State William H. Seward.

After he had shot the president, Booth's plan was to leap to the stage and dash out of the stage door into the alley outside, where he had arranged to have a horse waiting. He would then flee south, speeding across the Navy Yard Bridge and into Maryland.

Early that afternoon, Booth showed up at Mary Surratt's boardinghouse, just as Mary Surratt was making preparations to leave for Surrattsville. While she and Booth were talking, Weichmann left to hire the horse and buggy. When he returned, Booth and Mary Surratt were still in the parlor chatting.

After Booth left, Mary Surratt prepared to depart for Surrattsville. Just before getting into the buggy, Mary Surratt stopped and said, "Wait, Mr. Weichmann, I must get those things of Booth's."

She went back into the house and returned with a small package wrapped in string. The package contained a pair of field glasses. Mary Surratt told Weichmann that Booth had asked her to leave the package at the Surratt Tavern for him.

Later in the day, when Mary Surratt and Weichmann arrived at the Surratt Tavern, the widow went inside with the package. She asked for Nothey and was told that nobody knew where he was. When John Lloyd arrived, he was drunk and staggering. Mary Surratt handed him the package for Booth. Lloyd would later testify that Mary Surratt had said, "Hide this, for *tonight*."

Before leaving, Mary Surratt asked Lloyd whether he could repair a spring that had broken on her buggy. Despite his drunken state, Lloyd found a piece of rope and tied the spring so it would hold together. Then Mary Surratt and Weichmann headed back to Washington.

Later, at Mary Surratt's trial, her lawyer would argue that Lloyd was too drunk to be able to recall what Mary Surratt had said to him. But the prosecution answered by saying that he was clearminded enough to repair Mary Surratt's buggy without any problem.

Back at the boardinghouse, Mary Surratt and Weichmann had a late supper. Weichmann was in bed before 10 P.M. Shortly after, the widow kissed her daughter good night before turning off the kerosene lamps and retiring.

At about the same time that the lamps were being doused at the Surratt boardinghouse, John Wilkes Booth was carrying out his plan to assassinate the president at Ford's Theatre. And Lewis Paine, following Booth's orders, attacked Secretary of State William Seward, stabbing him and several members of his household staff. Seward managed to recover from his wounds. George

Atzerodt, assigned by Booth to assassinate Vice President Johnson, got drunk and never carried out his orders.

After his attack on Seward, Paine failed to escape from Washington. But Booth and David Herold, taking flight on horseback, were successful in crossing the Navy Yard Bridge into Maryland. They went straight to Surrattsville and the Surratt Tavern. There they got whiskey from John Lloyd and recovered one of the carbines that John Surratt had hidden about a month before.

Booth and Herold also picked up the neatly wrapped package containing Booth's field glasses that Mary Surratt had delivered that very afternoon.

On the twelfth day after the assassination, soldiers tracked Booth and Herold to a tobacco barn near Port Royal, Virginia, about sixty miles from Washington. Breaking orders to bring Booth back alive, a soldier fired a bullet that struck Booth in the back of the head. Within three hours, Booth was dead. Herold was captured and brought back to Washington.

The carbine and field glasses that Booth had picked up at the Surratt Tavern were recovered and would be used in the case the government was to build against Mary Surratt. Booth and Herold had left the second carbine in its hiding place at the Surratt Tavern. It would later be found and also be used as evidence against Mary Surratt.

There were dozens of witnesses at Ford's Theatre who identified Booth as the man who had assassinated Lincoln. A stableman, when questioned by police, linked John Surratt, Jr., David Herold, and George Atzerodt to Booth. Of the three, only John Surratt had a known address.

In the early morning hours following the assassination, Washington police paid a visit to Mrs. Surratt's boardinghouse on H Street.

When the police rang the front doorbell, they awakened Weichmann. He sleepily made his way down the darkened stairway and stood by the front door. "Who is it?" he asked.

"We're police," a voice came back. "Who are you?"

"Louis Weichmann."

"Is John Surratt in?"

"No. He is not in the city."

When Weichmann opened the door a crack, several policemen pushed their way inside. They were led by Detective John A. W. Clarvoe of the Washington police force. Once inside, the police officers went from room to room lighting the kerosene lamps.

Weichmann knocked on the door of Mrs. Surratt's bedroom. Detective Clarvoe stepped up to the door and asked, "Is this Mrs. Surratt?"

"Yes," the widow answered.

"I want to see John."

"John is not in the city, sir."

When the frightened Weichmann asked the detective to explain the meaning of the search and all the questions, the detective said, "Do you pretend

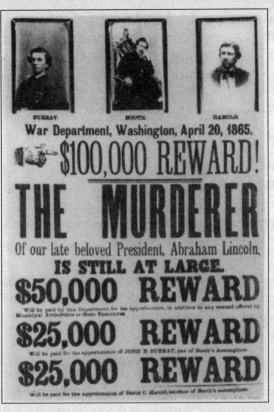

War Department, Washington, April 20, 1865.

$100,000 REWARD!

THE MURDERER

Of our late beloved President, Abraham Lincoln,

IS STILL AT LARGE.

$50,000 REWARD

Will be paid by this Department for his apprehension, in addition to any reward offered by Municipal Authorities or State Executives.

$25,000 REWARD

Will be paid for the apprehension of JOHN H SURRAT, one of Booth's Accomplices.

$25,000 REWARD

Will be paid for the apprehension of David C. Harold, another of Booth's accomplices.

Several different reward posters were issued in the days following Lincoln's assassination. John Surratt's and David Herold's names were both misspelled in this version.

to tell me that you do not know what happened this night?"

"I do. What happened?"

Then Clarvoe told Weichmann that President Lincoln had been assassinated by John Wilkes Booth, the actor.

"Great God!" said Weichmann. "I see it all now."

Mary Surratt was answering questions being put to her by another detective. Weichmann called out to her: "What do you think, Mrs. Surratt? President Lincoln has been murdered by John Wilkes Booth. . . ."

"My God! You don't tell me so!" Mary Surratt cried.

Clarvoe watched the reactions of Mary Surratt and Weichmann at the news. To him, they both seem deeply shocked.

Clarvoe and the other officers continued to ask Mary Surratt about her son, when she last saw him, where he might be. They also questioned Mary Surratt's daughter, Anna, and the other boarders. They searched the house from top to bottom. Unable to find anything suspicious, the police left.

The investigation of Lincoln's murder was headed by Edwin M. Stanton, Lincoln's Secretary of War, an ambitious man with many enemies. Even the president did not like him very much. After the shooting of the president, it was Stanton, not Vice President Johnson, who had taken over the reins of government. As doctors ministered to the mortally wounded Lincoln, Stanton wrote messages and issued orders.

It was Stanton's belief that the president was the victim of an enormous plot hatched by the Confederacy. He believed that John Wilkes Booth was a tool of Jefferson Davis and other Confederate leaders, and that hundreds of other terrorists were involved. Stanton wanted 150 police officers from the city of Washington, 500 military policemen, the U.S. Secret Service, and 8,000 soldiers stationed in and around Washington to begin seeking out, questioning, detaining, and arresting "these terrorists" at once.

Anyone who had the slightest connection with Booth was arrested and jailed. John T. Ford, the owner of the theater and close friend of Booth's, who had been in Richmond at the time of the assassination, and two of Ford's brothers were among those thrown into prison. John Wilkes Booth's brother, the noted actor Junius Brutus Booth, was arrested in Cincinnati, where he was appearing in a play, and returned to Washington. James Pumphrey, the stable owner from whom Booth had hired his horse, and John Lloyd, who had rented Mary Surratt's tavern in Maryland, were among the scores of others who were seized and imprisoned as suspects.

It didn't take long for Stanton's dragnet to snare Mary Surratt. On the Monday night following the assassination, a representative of Stanton's War Department and several officers showed up at Mary Surratt's house with orders to arrest her and anyone else living under her roof. That included Mary Surratt's sister, her daughter, Anna, and a young woman boarder.

As the officers and their captives were about to leave the house for waiting carriages, Lewis Paine suddenly appeared. He looked as if he had slept in the clothes he was wearing and he carried a heavy pickax over one shoulder. Paine explained that Mary Surratt had hired him to dig a well and he had come to ask what time she wanted him to begin work in the morning.

The officers asked Mary Surratt if she knew the young man. "Before God," Mary Surratt declared, "I never saw him before." That answer was to count heavily against Mary Surratt in the weeks that were to follow.

During her trial, the prosecution sought to establish that Mary Surratt did indeed know Paine. Mary Surratt's lawyers would argue, however, that she could not be blamed for failing to recognize him. In his visits, Paine had sometimes worn a fake mustache to confuse her and her guests. Other times he played the role of a Baptist minister. On still other occasions, Paine said he was so ill that he could not join the other boarders in the dining room at mealtime and asked to have his meals served in his room.

Eventually, Stanton singled out eight suspects who were to be tried as conspirators. In addition to Mary Surratt, they were

- Lewis Paine (né Powell), one of Booth's original conspirators and the man who brutally attacked Secretary of State Seward and his son, Frederick.
- David Herold, who joined Booth at the Navy Yard Bridge after the assassination and fled

into Maryland with him. He surrendered to authorities after Booth had been shot.

- George Atzerodt, along with Herold and Paine, closely linked to Booth and the conspiracy from the beginning.
- Edward (Ned) Spangler, a carpenter and scene shifter at Ford's Theatre, who was thought to have aided Booth in the frantic moments following the shooting.
- Samuel Arnold and Michael O'Laughlin, old school friends of Booth's, who were involved in the actor's original plan to kidnap Lincoln.
- Dr. Samuel A. Mudd, who sheltered Booth at his home near Bryantown, Maryland, and treated the leg the actor had broken in leaping from the president's box to the Ford's Theatre stage.

There was to be no trial by jury for the accused. Once the government authorities had the eight suspects behind bars, President Andrew Johnson signed an executive order that provided they were to be tried by a military commission of seven generals and two colonels. A military trial was judged to be proper since Lincoln, the Commander in Chief of the armed forces, was killed while the country was at war.

The eight prisoners got harsh treatment, thanks to orders from Secretary Stanton. He instructed that, except for Mary Surratt, each be made to wear a heavy canvas hood that was to be tied about the neck. While a small hole was provided for breathing and eating, the prisoners could not see or hear.

Paine and Atzerodt each had one leg chained to a heavy iron ball. It took two guards to lift each ball from the floor. The other prisoners, including Mary Surratt, had their feet chained together.

In addition, the male prisoners were made to wear shackles. Mary Surratt's hands were free.

Dr. George Loring Porter, the prison doctor, concerned about the health of the prisoners, felt he had to protest and went to see Stanton. "The brutality with which the prisoners are being treated must be modified," Dr. Porter said. "The constant pressure of those thickly padded hoods may induce insanity."

Stanton was not moved.

"The hot summer weather is coming on," Dr. Porter continued. "The lack of sanitary facilities, such as bathing, contributes to their suffering. They also need daily exercise."

Stanton indicated he might provide some measure of relief, but conditions never changed.

Except for Mary Surratt, who was held in Old Capitol Prison (where the Supreme Court Building is now located), the so-called conspirators were confined to the third floor of an old prison building, today known as Quarters 20 at Fort Lesley McNair in Washington.

Each prisoner was placed in a cell with an

empty cell on each side. This prevented the prisoners from communicating with one another.

Thomas B. Florence, editor of the *Daily Constitutional*, took a special interest in Mary Surratt and her plight. He noted that she had been arrested in April, when the weather was cool, and was still wearing winter clothing in the summer's heat. "She was conferred to an inner cell of the prison," he wrote, "the dimensions of which were about seven feet long and three feet wide. It had a stone floor, stone walls, and an iron-grated door." Brigadier General William E. Doster, a lawyer for the two defendants, said the cell was "scarcely habitable."

Mary Surratt's ordeal finally caused Colonel William P. Wood, superintendent of the prison, to speak to his friend Stanton, and ask for an improvement in conditions. Stanton promised to do what he could but only if Mary Surratt agreed to furnish information about Booth and places he might have used as hideouts in the days after the assassination.

But Stanton had no intention of making good on his promise. As soon as Mary Surratt had disclosed what little she knew, Stanton ordered her transferred from Wood's control at Old Capitol Prison to Quarters 20 at Fort McNair.

The trial of the eight accused began on May 9, 1865, in a stifling hot courtroom that was but a short walk from the prisoners' cells. More than 400 witnesses were heard before the proceedings finally drew to a close on June 30. In all those weeks, none of the prisoners was allowed to take the witness stand and say a word in his or her defense.

Mary Surratt had a skilled lawyer in Reverdy Johnson, a Maryland senator and a former U.S. attorney general. But the prosecution objected to Johnson, saying that as a senator he "did not recognize the moral obligation of an oath of loyalty" to the government. Johnson managed to turn aside that challenge, but other attacks on his integrity eventually forced him to step down. He handed over the defense of Mary Surratt to younger and less experienced lawyers.

During the trial, the prisoners sat in a row on a raised platform at one end of the courtroom facing the military commission. A soldier stood beside each of the accused. Mary Surratt, dressed in black, with a heavy black veil over her head and face, sat at the far left, a few feet removed from the others. She was given an armchair while the others sat in straight chairs.

Throughout the trial, Mary Surratt protested that she knew nothing of the plotting that went on at her boardinghouse. The government had only the flimsiest evidence to offer that she was aware of the conspiracy.

The officers who took Mary Surratt into custody testified that in her living room was a framed picture of three young women who represented "Spring, Summer, and Autumn." Within the frame behind the picture, an officer had discovered a small photograph of John Wilkes Booth. On the dresser in Mary Surratt's bedroom, the officers recovered two bullet molds. It was never made clear how these items were a link between Mary Surratt and Booth's plot to assassinate the president.

One of the officers called to the witness stand was asked to identify Mary Surratt as the woman he had arrested at the boardinghouse. The officer said that he could not see her face. Then, according to the court stenographer's account, "slowly, cooly, Mrs. Surratt lifted her veil, looked steadily at him, and slowly, cooly lowered her veil again." In such instances, Mary Surratt was said to earn the admiration of courthouse visitors for her "great nerve."

Secretary Stanton decided who would testify against the suspects, and bribed some of them with promises that they would not be prosecuted in exchange for what they said. John Lloyd and Louis Weichmann were two of the government's key witnesses. Each played a crucial role in sending Mary Surratt to the gallows.

On the night of the assassination, when Booth and Herold stopped at Surrattsville, Lloyd had given them whiskey and one of the carbines. Despite the fact that Stanton had announced that any person who aided the conspirators in their escape would face the death penalty, Lloyd never became one of the accused. Instead of being held as a suspect, he became a witness.

Lloyd testified that John Surratt, David Herold, and George Atzerodt had come to the tavern several weeks before the assassination and left two rifles, ammunition, and some supplies.

Then, on the Tuesday before the assassination, Mary Surratt had paid a visit, Lloyd told the court. He said she asked him about "the things."

"I did not know what she had referred to," Lloyd said. "Then she came out plainer and asked me about the 'shooting irons.' She told me to get them ready, that they would be wanted soon."

Lloyd said that he saw Mary Surratt again just three days later. "She told me to have those shooting irons ready that night," he testified, "There would be some parties that would call for them."

Lloyd also said that Mary Surratt gave him a package wrapped in brown paper. He peeked into it and saw that it contained field glasses.

Louis Weichmann's testimony was just as damaging to Mary Surratt. According to evidence that was produced after the trial, Stanton had scared Weichmann to death by telling him that he was just as guilty as Mary Surratt, her son John, and the others who visited the boardinghouse and that he would have to pay the penalty. Like Lloyd, Weichmann testified to save himself.

Weichmann told the court that he had seen Booth at the boardinghouse on several occasions. He testified how on the afternoon of April 14, Booth came to see Mary Surratt and gave her a package containing field glasses to be dropped off at the tavern.

Weichmann testified that after driving Mary Surratt to the tavern and delivering the package, he heard the widow tell Lloyd to have the shooting irons and whiskey ready, that they would be called for that very night.

Mary Surratt's defenders portrayed her as a good woman, a good mother. It was her misfortune, they said, to have been in the wrong place at the wrong time.

When questioned in prison before the trial, Mary Surratt was asked, "Did your son or Mr. Booth or Port Tobacco [the nickname used by George Atzerodt] ever tell you that they engaged in a plot to kill the president?"

"Never in the world," replied Mary Surratt, "if it was the last word I have ever to utter."

Did Mary Surratt conspire with John Wilkes Booth in his plot to murder the president? It is not likely. She may have been aware of Booth's earlier plan to kidnap Lincoln, although there is no direct evidence that she did.

Unfortunately for Mary Surratt and the others, the court made no distinction between Booth's plot to kidnap the president and his plan to assassinate him. Involvement with one was considered to be involvement with the other.

While no proof was ever presented that Mary Surratt ever did anything more than perform a few errands for Booth, the military court did not believe that she went to Surrattsville only on business matters, to collect money owed her. Meeting secretly, the panel voted the death penalty for Mary Surratt. Hanging was the means of execution in those days.

Paine, Atzerodt, and Herold were also to be hanged. Dr. Mudd, Arnold, and O'Laughlin were given life in prison at hard labor; Spangler's sentence was six years at hard labor.

Attached to the final page of their recommendations, the commissioners asked for mercy in the case of Mary Surratt, that her sentence be changed to life imprisonment. President Johnson signed the order for execution on July 5. He insisted for the rest of his life that Judge Advocate General Joseph Holt had never shown him the recommendation for mercy for Mary Surratt.

Holt denied this, saying he had seen the president read it. Furthermore, said Judge Holt, Johnson had told him that he believed Mary Surratt should be executed "because she had kept the nest that hatched the egg."

On July 6, Mary Surratt and the three others were told of their sentences and that they were to be hanged the very next day. The government was wasting no time.

Anna Surratt became hysterical when she heard the news. Weeping uncontrollably, she rushed to the White House and begged to see President Johnson and ask for his mercy on behalf of her mother.

She was kept from her mission by Preston King, the president's closest friend, and Senator James Lane of Kansas, among others. They blocked the stairs to the president's quarters, saying he was ill. Anna went back to the prison, where she was al-

A general view of the prison yard as final preparations were being made for the execution of the conspirators.

lowed to sleep in the cell with her mother on the final night of her life.

A gallows had been erected in the prison yard and the executioner had tested it. On the morning of July 7, a burning hot and sultry day, the four prisoners were led out of their cells and up the thirteen steps to the scaffold.

Mary Surratt sagged and swayed and had to be supported on each side by an officer. Two priests walked ahead of her. An officer held an umbrella over her head to shield her from the sun.

All four of the condemned were made to stand

as the order of the execution was read. Then their hands were drawn behind them and tied and their legs were bound together. White hoods were put over their heads and the nooses were placed about their necks and tightened.

On a signal, supporting posts were knocked away from the front part of the platform, and it swung down on hinges. The four bodies plunged downward about five feet. Mary Surratt was thought to have died instantly, for her body swung quietly.

"Rush to judgment" is a phrase that has been used in connection with the murder of John F. Kennedy. It refers to the great haste in which Lee Harvey Oswald was branded as Kennedy's assassin. O. J. Simpson's lawyers also used the phrase to describe the undue speed with which the Los Angeles Police Department decided the former football star to be guilty of killing his former wife.

Mary Surratt was convicted of a crime — conspiracy to murder the president — in which her guilt was never really proven. There was reasonable doubt. Mary Surratt was the victim of a vengeful government's "rush to judgment."

As for Mary Surratt's son John, he was in upstate New York at the time of the assassination. When he heard the news of Lincoln's murder, he fled to Montreal, Canada, and remained in hiding there during his mother's trial. Friends told him that the government had no real evidence against his mother and that she was being held captive in an effort to lure him out of hiding.

After his mother's execution, John made his way to Europe. Authorities of the United States eventually arrested him in Italy. John escaped, only to be arrested again in Alexandria, Egypt.

After being brought back to the United States, John was tried in a civil court, not before a military tribunal. The court was presented with the same evidence and heard many of the same witnesses as in the earlier conspiracy trial. But the jury could not agree on a verdict, and John was released.

John later married, fathered seven children, and lived a quiet life as an accountant for a Baltimore steamship line. He died in 1916, without ever revealing what dealings he and his mother might actually have had with John Wilkes Booth.

5
Incident at West Point

Johnson Chesnut Whittaker was a man ahead of his time — way ahead.

Born on the Chesnut Plantation in Camden, South Carolina, the son of a slave mother and a freedman father, Johnson Whittaker was one of the first black men to win an appointment to the United States Military Academy at West Point.

Getting accepted proved to be the easy part for Whittaker. Succeeding as a student in the face of the overwhelming obstacles that were placed in his path proved impossible.

Because of his color, the other cadets made him an outcast. No one spoke to him except to give orders. No one ever visited his room nor was he ever invited to visit anyone else's. No one would sit next to him in the mess hall or stand next to him at formation.

Johnson Whittaker became a West Point cadet in 1876.

The hellish treatment got even worse. One night as Whittaker lay sleeping, three masked men burst into his dormitory room. They slashed his hands and ears with a razor, set fire to pages they ripped from his Bible, and left him tied to his bed, unconscious.

Incredibly, the authorities at West Point, instead of seeking out his attackers, accused Whittaker of staging the incident. Court-martialed and found guilty, Whittaker never received his second-lieutenant's commission and was forced to leave the Academy in disgrace. Only in recent years has the Whittaker family managed to receive some measure of justice.

Through the early years of his life, Johnson Whittaker worked hard to achieve success.

His mother was a "body slave" to Mary Chesnut, who became famous for her revealing portrayal of plantation life through her Civil War diaries. Whittaker's father, who left the plantation shortly after Johnson was born, worked as a tailor to earn his son's freedom.

It was impressed upon Whittaker at a very early age that only through education could he hope to achieve acceptance. Whittaker studied privately with Richard Greener, the first African American to graduate from Harvard College. Whittaker later attended the University of South Carolina, then a freedmen's school.

Congressman S. L. Hoge agreed to appoint Whittaker to the U.S. Military Academy in 1876. At the time, West Point was a deeply troubled institution, reflecting what was happening in the nation as a whole.

After the Civil War ended in 1865, slavery was abolished and black Americans gained their civil rights during a period known as Reconstruction. But then the pendulum began to swing the other way. By the late 1870s blacks had lost many of the rights they had gained and were again suffering from widespread segregation and poverty.

Whittaker was nominated by Congressman Hoge to fill an opening at West Point that had been created by the departure of black cadet James Webster Smith. Like Whittaker, Smith was "separated from the corps by a wall of prejudice," as one writer described it. After four years at West Point, Smith was dismissed for academic reasons.

Unlike Smith, who sometimes clashed with white cadets, Whittaker learned to steel himself against the isolation and insults. He made friends with other blacks, including Louis Simpson and Walter Mitchell, both of whom were servants at West Point. Occasionally, he visited a settlement of black families in nearby Highland Falls.

During vacation periods, Whittaker once called upon a friend, Moses Wester, a janitor in New York City. Another time, he went to Washington to spend time with his former teacher, Richard Greener.

Whittaker spent most of his time at West Point studying, writing letters to his mother and friends, and reading the Bible. The Bible gave him strength. He underlined passages that had special meaning to him and wrote eloquent comments in the margins. On April 21, 1878, on the front leaf of his Bible, he wrote: "Try never to injure another by word, by action . . . Forgive as soon as you are injured and forget as soon as you forgive."

Most of the passages that Whittaker underlined related to loneliness. One was from the Gospel According to John, chapter sixteen, verse thirty-two: "Yet I am not alone, because the Father is with me." In the margin next to the verse, he wrote: "I in my dreary solitude, surrounded by none but enemies, can say that I am not destitute of friends for God is near me."

During his nearly four years at West Point, Whittaker had been an average student. Although he was repeating some subjects, he was in no danger of failure. One of his professors described him as "very studious and very attentive."

Whittaker's situation at West Point became more troublesome when, on the evening of Sunday, April 4, 1880, he returned to his room after dinner to find a small envelope addressed to "Cadet Whittaker." Inside was a handwritten note:

Mr. Whittaker
You will be fixed. Better keep awake.
A friend

The twenty-one-year-old Whittaker didn't know what to make of the note. Was it some kind of a joke or should he consider it a serious threat? While Whittaker had learned to resign himself to the rejection and isolation, the note bothered him because it suggested physical violence. He could not stop thinking about it.

Whittaker decided he would speak to Louis Simpson, the black attendant at the West Point bathhouse, about the note. Simpson read it, then shrugged. He told Whittaker that while it indeed

"You will be fixed" warned the handwritten note that Whittaker found in his room.

might be a warning, if he showed it to anyone in authority he would only be laughed at.

Whittaker still didn't know what to do. By the next day, however, he had apparently made up his mind, for in a letter to his mother, Whittaker said he was planning to show the note to General John M. Schofield, the superintendent of the Academy.

Whittaker never got a chance. On Monday night, after a typical day of classes, Whittaker returned to his room, studied, and read his Bible. He went to bed soon after midnight.

Sometime during the early morning hours, while it was still dark, Whittaker was abruptly awakened when he felt somebody pounce on top of him. Then he was seized by the throat and choked. Someone else punched him about the head and his nose started bleeding. By this time,

Whittaker realized there were three men in his room. All three wore dark clothing and masks. They struck Whittaker about the head, and one of the attackers warned him, "Speak now and you are a dead man. Don't you holler."

The three men dragged Whittaker to the floor. He heard one of them say, "Let's mark him the way we mark hogs down South." The men then slashed Whittaker's ear lobes, the way Southern farmers slash the ears of pigs before slaughtering them. When they had finished, one of the men took a pair of scissors and snipped out clumps of Whittaker's hair.

The terrified Whittaker tried to fight off the trio of attackers but when he reached out for them he was cut on the left hand. His hands were tied in front of him. One of the assailants, noting the blood streaming from Whittaker's nose and ears, said, "Look out, don't hurt him. See how much he bleeds. . . ." Then he placed a handkerchief over one of Whittaker's bleedings ears.

One of the men picked up a small mirror, held it in front of Whittaker's face, and made him look at his image. He then struck poor Whittaker on the forehead with the mirror, which shattered.

Before leaving, the trio took strips of white belting worn by cadets and tied Whittaker's legs to the rails of his cot. "Cry out or speak of this affair and you are a dead man," Whittaker was told again. Then the men left.

Whittaker immediately called for help but his voice was weak and no one heard him. He wanted

120

to shout louder but he was afraid his attackers would hear him and return as they had threatened. Exhausted and trembling, Whittaker lay helpless on the floor. Finally, he passed out.

Not long after daybreak, when the cadets lined up for roll call, it was quickly discovered that Whittaker was missing. Major Alexander Piper, the officer in charge, ordered George Burnett, the cadet officer of the day, to check Whittaker's room. Burnett hurried to Whittaker's barracks and up the four flights of stairs leading to his room.

He pounded on the door. When there was no answer, he opened the door and looked in. Burnett gasped at what he saw. Whittaker, wearing only his underclothes, was lying on the floor, his legs tied to the railing of his cot. He was covered with blood. The room was a mess.

Burnett made no effort to help Whittaker but ran to get Major Piper. He first alerted Cadet Frederick Hodgson, who occupied the room across the hall from Whittaker's. "Look! Look!" Burnett cried.

Hodgson peered in. "I believe he's dead," he said.

When Burnett returned to Whittaker's room with Major Piper, Whittaker was still unconscious. Piper checked Whittaker's pulse and found it normal. Using scissors that he found on the floor, Burnett cut the belting to free Whittaker's legs and hands.

Whittaker remained flat on the floor, his eyes shut, showing no sign of consciousness.

Piper sent for Major Charles Alexander, the Academy doctor. Dr. Alexander had a reputation for dealing harshly with "goldbrickers," cadets who tried to fake illness in an effort to avoid duties or work.

When Dr. Alexander arrived and checked Whittaker's pulse, his brow wrinkled. "There's nothing wrong here," he said.

Dr. Alexander examined Whittaker for head injuries and other wounds. Bending over the victim, he said, "What is wrong with you? I want to know what to do for you."

Whittaker did not move and his eyes remained closed. Then his lips moved. "Oh, don't cut me. I never hurt you," he said softly.

"We're not going to hurt you," Dr. Alexander replied. "What is the matter with you?"

"Please don't cut me," Whittaker repeated in a weak voice. His eyes remained closed.

Dr. Alexander tried to rouse Whittaker by shaking him and pinching him. He drew back one of Whittaker's eyelids and examined the pupil. Whittaker showed no response.

When Lieutenant Colonel Henry M. Lazelle, the commandant of cadets, arrived on the scene, Dr. Alexander told him that he thought Whittaker might be faking unconsciousness and that he was "not so badly hurt as he tried to make out."

Lazelle stared down at Whittaker's motionless form and said, "Get up, Mr. Whittaker; be a man." At the same time, Dr. Alexander began shaking him again.

"Get up, Mr. Whittaker. Get up, sir," Colonel Lazelle repeated. "Open your eyes."

Whittaker stirred and opened his eyes, then sat up. He said nothing. When Dr. Alexander ordered him to get to his feet, he did so. He then walked groggily to the washstand in his room and began to wash the blood from his face.

Dr. Alexander asked Whittaker to sit down so he could treat his injuries. When Dr. Alexander asked for an explanation of what had happened, Whittaker gave him a detailed account of the attack.

Dr. Alexander seemed skeptical. He kept questioning Whittaker, attempting to disprove his story. But Whittaker gave clear and reasonable answers to every question.

As Dr. Alexander was treating Whittaker, General Schofield, the West Point superintendent, appeared. Rumors were circulating that Whittaker had been seriously hurt and perhaps killed. Major Piper was quick to assure the general that all was well. "It's not as bad as we thought," Piper declared.

Schofield nodded. Then he glanced at Whittaker and asked about his injuries. Before leaving the scene, the general ordered Colonel Lazelle to investigate the incident and prepare a full report as quickly as possible.

Lazelle began by questioning Whittaker as he was washing and dressing. Lazelle ordered the room be put in order and all of the bloodstained clothing be washed. Later, those who questioned the honesty of the army's investigation would cite

Lazelle's order as evidence of bad faith, for it had caused the destruction of important evidence.

Early that evening, Whittaker was made to undergo another physical examination, this one conducted by Dr. Henry Lippencott, an assistant to Dr. Alexander. General Schofield and Colonel Lazelle were both present as Dr. Lippencott probed Whittaker's injuries, one by one.

Dr. Lippencott agreed with Dr. Alexander that Whittaker had been slashed on both ears, sustaining a wound that was "five-eighths of an inch long on the right ear lobe, and one slightly shorter on the left." They both found a "thin scratch" on Whittaker's left hand and two small cuts on the top of the toe of his left foot. They found that his hair had been crudely cut "in swaths." And they estimated Whittaker had lost no more than two ounces of blood.

On Lazelle's orders, Lieutenant William H. Coffin visited Whittaker's room several times on the day of the attack and the day after. He took several items, including a black necktie, a pair of scissors, a pen knife, and Whittaker's Bible. Coffin also sifted through Whittaker's letters and his personal effects.

Whittaker did not object. He willingly handed over whatever Coffin asked for.

Whittaker must have suspected by now that the humiliation and physical blows he had suffered were the least of his problems, for he was being treated more like a suspect than a victim. The authorities at West Point and what they might be planning to do were what really worried him.

On Wednesday morning, less than forty-eight hours after the attack, Whittaker's worst fears were confirmed when Lazelle delivered his report to General Schofield. All of the evidence, Colonel Lazelle declared, pointed to the conclusion that Whittaker had faked the attack. He had written the note of warning himself, mutilated his own body, tied himself up, and faked being unconscious.

After reading the report, General Schofield called Whittaker to his office. The general was an imposing figure, tall and stout, his face ringed with a thick growth of side whiskers. He could boast a long and distinguished army career. During the Civil War, he had commanded forces that balked Confederate General John Hood's invasion of Tennessee and he later served with General William Tecumseh Sherman in one of the war's final campaigns. He had been named superintendent of the Military Academy in 1876.

Several other officers were present when Whittaker entered the general's office. He saluted and took a seat.

"It appears from the report, from the investigation," General Schofield declared, "that you did this thing yourself."

Whittaker sat in stunned silence. Citing the evidence that had been collected, General Schofield said there was no reason to believe that Whittaker had sustained a blow that had left him unconscious. Further, it appeared that he had cut himself, not been someone's victim, the general said. Also, the handwriting of the warning note closely resembled his own.

The general continued, saying that he could have freed himself from the flimsy belting used to tie his feet with "a vigorous kick or two," and, although he had not been gagged, he did not cry out for help.

Whittaker could hardly believe his ears. How could he be accused of a crime that others had committed against him? Whittaker could feel a wave of anger and resentment rising up inside him.

But Whittaker managed to control his rage. When the general asked him to respond, Whittaker calmly asked that an official court of inquiry be called into session to weigh the facts in the case and deliver an opinion.

"You are entitled to a court of inquiry," said General Schofield, "and you most certainly shall have one."

By the time the court of inquiry was called into session on April 9, 1880, just five days after the attack, the case had become a national sensation. There were debates in the U.S. Senate as to whether those in charge at West Point were prejudiced in their treatment of black cadets.

Major newspapers of the day assigned reporters to cover the hearings, which were held in the

Academy library, and gave front-page treatment to their stories. From the first day, the room assigned to the inquiry was filled with spectators, many of them wives of West Point officers.

Before and during the inquiry, General Schofield granted several newspapers interviews in which the West Point superintendent branded poor Whittaker as the one who had committed the crime.

General Schofield declared that there was no evidence to link any of the other cadets to the attack. Whittaker himself was the guilty party. He had mutilated himself, the general said, so it would be necessary for him to spend some time in the hospital. He would thereby be absent from final examinations, which he feared he would not pass. General Schofield added that most West Point officers shared this belief.

Four West Point officers were named to carry out the investigation. The team was headed by Lieutenant Clinton Sears, an assistant professor, whose role was much like that of a prosecuting attorney.

Whittaker was defended by First Lieutenant John G. D. Knight, also an assistant professor. It was a difficult assignment for him. Knight was, after all, a member of the West Point community. He fully realized that his performance would have a bearing on his career, his future.

On the first day of the hearing, Whittaker was called to the stand to explain what had happened on, what one biographer termed, "his night of horror." The black cadet told how he had been assaulted by three masked men, cut and slashed, and left with his legs and arms tied.

Whittaker was then questioned about the attack. The questioning continued the next day. Whittaker spoke clearly and firmly and gave logical answers to the questions put to him, making a favorable impression upon the court.

But later doubts were cast upon Whittaker's version of events by George Burnett, the cadet officer of the day who was the first to enter Whittaker's room following the attack. Whittaker and Burnett had never been on the best of terms. Further, Burnett was one of the cadets that some people suspected as being one of Whittaker's attackers.

Burnett seemed eager to testify. When asked how Whittaker had been tied, he got down onto the floor to show how Whittaker's body had been positioned. Then he demonstrated how Whittaker might have easily tied himself to his cot, using an iron bedstead that had been brought into the hearing room.

Unfortunately for Whittaker, he was not present in the courtroom when Burnett testified. At Lieutenant Knight's suggestion, he had returned to his classes. He, therefore, was unable to point out errors in Burnett's testimony and bring them to the attention of the court.

Lieutenant Sears called several witnesses to the stand to testify concerning the handwritten note of warning that Whittaker had received. Although they lacked training in handwriting analysis,

128

Sears called these witnesses "handwriting experts."

Samples of Whittaker's handwriting were mixed in with a number of samples of the handwriting of other cadets, and then all the samples were compared to the handwriting on the note. According to Sears, the "experts" found Whittaker's handwriting and that of the warning note to be identical.

Sears also claimed that one of the experts was able to match one edge of the warning note with the edge of a letter that Whittaker had written to his mother. To Sears, this was evidence that both had come from the same piece of paper. Sears was thus able to conclude that the warning note had been written by Whittaker.

Sears called Whittaker to the stand and asked him whether he had written the note. "No!" Whittaker declared. Then how did he explain the experts' findings, Sears wanted to know. Whittaker said that perhaps the note had been forged.

In the midst of the hearings, *The New York Times* added to the drama with a feature story that exploded Sears' version of the case. According to the newspaper, rumors were circulating in the nearby village of Highland Falls that on the night before the attack three cadets had been overheard in a local tavern plotting to get rid of the black cadet. When the story became widespread, West Point officers were said to have visited the tavern keeper and told him to keep quiet about the incident.

Although the article in the *Times* did not mention the tavern keeper by name, the people of Highland Falls were convinced it was Philip Ryan. Ryan's Tavern was a cadet hangout.

The article in *The New York Times* served to shift the spotlight from Whittaker to other cadets. When called to testify, several cadets in Whittaker's class admitted to having been out on the night of the attack, although all of them seemed able to convince investigators they were elsewhere at the time the attack occurred. Other cadets admitted being patrons of Ryan's Tavern.

The article and the questions it raised gave Whittaker's cause a boost. No longer could he be considered the one and only suspect in the case. Other cadets could just as easily be guilty.

The court of inquiry continued through April and deep into May. More handwriting experts were called to bolster Sears' case. A Charleston, South Carolina, newspaper pointed out that even if Whittaker had written the warning note himself, it did not mean that he was the perpetrator.

In his closing statement, Lieutenant Sears said there "was not a scrap of evidence . . . to show that any cadet save Whittaker was in any way connected with this assault." His motive was clear, said Sears: ". . . to get into the hospital and avoid study for the time or gain the sympathy of instructors and thus get through the approaching examinations."

Lieutenant Knight's summation lacked the vigor that Sears had displayed. He did say that there was no reason to believe that Whittaker was lying, and that he really had no motive to do what he was accused of doing. If he wanted to miss an exam, there were better ways of doing it than slashing one's earlobes.

Once the closing statements were completed, it did not take the members of the court of inquiry very long to announce their findings. The very next day, the court declared Whittaker to be the guilty party. It said that he had written the note of warning, inflicted the "slight wounds" upon himself, and faked being unconscious.

Whittaker was crushed by the court's decision. "My heart droops in despair and life seems almost a burden," he said in a letter to Professor Greener. As he wrote, he said, tears were running down his face. His greatest concern was for his mother. He said that he could not bear to tell her of the court's verdict.

Whittaker returned to classes. But the burden of the trial and its outcome weighed heavily upon him, and his grades nosedived. He did manage, however, to get passing marks in all of his subjects except philosophy.

Meanwhile, Professor Greener and other of Whittaker's supporters had launched a campaign calling for Whittaker to be court-martialed as a means of clearing his name. Whittaker himself, in December 1880, wrote to President Rutherford B. Hayes to declare that his trial had been unjust and was filled with "false and malicious accusations." He asked for a court-martial as a method of obtaining justice.

The president seemed impressed with Whittaker's letter. Not long after, he ordered the court-martial. It began on February 3, 1881, in the Army Building in New York City. Six of the ten officers who made up the court were non-West Pointers, which was considered an advantage for Whittaker.

This time Whittaker was defended by a skilled and experienced courtroom lawyer, Daniel H. Chamberlain, a former governor of South Carolina.

The court-martial was very much a replay of the court of inquiry. The most notable piece of new evidence presented by the prosecution was a claim by a handwriting expert that he had discovered "underwriting" on the warning note.

According to his testimony, this underwriting, which was made up of words that had been partially erased, could be seen only under a microscope. It was additional evidence, he said, that the warning note and a letter of Whittaker's to his mother had been written on the same sheet of paper.

Chamberlain ridiculed these findings. There was no underwriting, he stated, and he called experts to support his belief. He also offered proof that the torn edge of the warning note did not match the edge of Whittaker's letter to his mother. They were not even written on the same type of paper, Chamberlain pointed out.

In his closing statement, Chamberlain declared that the government's handwriting experts were unqualified bunglers. He challenged the testimony of the two doctors who had examined Whittaker, pointing out they had not even been able to agree to where Whittaker's wounds were located.

Chamberlain also said that it was absurd to think that anyone could have tied himself up as securely as Whittaker had been when he was found. He went on to establish that Whittaker could not have cut his own hair, for no scissors had been found that could have done the job.

The government had not even introduced any real motive, Chamberlain said. It made no sense to suggest that Whittaker would mutilate his body in April in order to miss an exam that was to be given in June.

Chamberlain also reminded the court that it was not up to Whittaker to prove his innocence. It was the government's task to prove him guilty. Suspicion was not enough.

When Chamberlain finished his summation, the courtroom spectators applauded loudly. Major Asa Bird Gardiner then offered the closing statement for the government. He recounted the entire incident, claiming the government's case was supported by two civilian witnesses, seven commissioned officers, and numerous cadets.

Daniel Chamberlain's brilliant defense made little or no impact upon the tribunal. On June 10, 1881, the court delivered its verdict: Whittaker was guilty as charged.

The board ruled that he was to be dishonorably discharged from the Military Academy, fined one dollar, and sentenced to a year in prison at hard labor. The prison sentence was later canceled.

Two years after Whittaker was drummed out of West Point, President Chester Alan Arthur reversed the court-martial decision.

But the president's decision didn't change things for Whittaker. On the very same day, Secretary of War Robert Todd Lincoln, son of President Abraham Lincoln, signed an order that served to dismiss Whittaker from the Military Academy. The reason: Whittaker was said to have failed an oral exam in natural philosophy.

After he left the Military Academy, Whittaker returned to South Carolina and led a successful life. He told only a few people about his misfortunes as a West Point cadet. He went back to school, earning a law degree from the University of South Carolina.

For a time, Whittaker practiced law in Sumter, South Carolina. He later turned to teaching at the Colored Normal Industrial, Agricultural and Mechanical College in Orangeburg, South Carolina. The institution later became South Carolina State College.

Whittaker married and had two sons, Miller and John. Both were commissioned officers in the army during World War I. Miller Whittaker later became president of South Carolina State College. John Whittaker moved to Detroit to work for Henry Ford, founder of the Ford Motor Company. Their children — Johnson Whittaker's grandchildren — became doctors and lawyers, and one served in

Many years after his court-martial, Johnson Whittaker (far right) posed with other members of the faculty at Colored Normal Industrial, Agricultural, and Mechanical College of South Carolina.

World War II as a member of the Tuskegee Airmen, the first black fighter pilots in the Army Air Force.

Johnson Whittaker died in 1931. He was buried in Orangeburg, South Carolina. He died without ever realizing his ambition of earning an army commission as a second lieutenant.

Several decades passed, and then Whittaker's name was in the news again. In 1972, John

Marszalek, a professor of history at Mississippi State University, happened to come upon a reference to the Whittaker case while doing research for a book about General William T. Sherman.

Marszalek came to realize that all blacks who attended West Point after the Civil War were poorly treated but that Whittaker's case stood out. It was one of "absolute horror," said Marszalek, who put aside his book about Sherman to dig into the Whittaker story.

In the National Archives in Washington, Marszalek found a 10,000-page handwritten transcript of Whittaker's court-martial. He also discovered Whittaker's Bible and many of his personal documents. From this material, Marszalek wrote a biography of Whittaker. Published in 1972, the book is titled *Court-martial: The Army vs. Johnson Whittaker*.

More decades passed. In 1994, the book became the basis of a cable television movie titled *Assault at West Point: The Court-martial of Johnson C. Whittaker*.

The Whittaker story then came to the attention of Senator Ernest F. Hollings of South Carolina. Senator Hollings introduced legislation in the Senate that would serve to award an army commission to Whittaker. The senator said that he was seeking "to right a wrong."

Representative James Clyburn of South Carolina introduced similar legislation in the House of Representatives. Togo West, the secretary of the

President Bill Clinton greets Cecil Whittaker Pequette, grand-daughter of Johnson Whittaker, at a White House ceremony in 1995 during which the president awarded Whittaker an Army commission.

army, agreed that Whittaker deserved a commission and urged President Bill Clinton to grant it.

So it was that on July 24, 1995, in a simple ceremony held in the Roosevelt Room of the White House, President Clinton gave the gold-plated bars of a second lieutenant to the descendants of Johnson Chesnut Whittaker. The president said: "Johnson Whittaker was a rare individual, a pathfinder — a man who, through courage, example, and perseverance, paved the way for future generations of African-American military leaders: General Chappie James, Lieutenant General Benjamin O. Davis — who is with us today — General Colin Powell, and so many others.

"We cannot undo history," the President continued. "But today, finally, we can pay tribute to a great American and we can acknowledge a great injustice."

President Clinton also presented Johnson Whittaker's Bible to Cecil Whittaker Pequette of Los Angeles, Whittaker's seventy-seven-year-old granddaughter. She was the only living relative who knew Whittaker. She was thirteen when he died. The Bible had been seized as evidence for Whittaker's court-martial in 1881 and had been stored in the National Archives for 114 years.

"The Bible was given to him by his mother when he went to West Point," Mrs. Pequette recalled, "and it . . . had been a comfort to him during his ordeal." Mrs. Pequette said she planned to donate the Bible to South Carolina State College, where it would be put on exhibition.

"This is a happy day, a proud day," Mrs. Pequette said following the White House ceremony. "It was also a day long in coming."

For Further Reading

Chapter 1: A Fight for Justice

Barthel, Joan. *A Death in Canaan*. New York: Dutton, 1976.

Connery, Donald S., editor. *Convicting the Innocent*. Cambridge, Massachusetts: Brookline Books, 1996.

Connery, Donald S. *Guilty Until Proven Innocent*. New York: G. P. Putnam, 1977.

Keiffer, Elisabeth. "We Always Knew Peter Didn't Kill His Mother." *Good Housekeeping* (July 1976) 77, 122–26.

Chapter 2: Shoot-out at Pine Ridge

Matthiessen, Peter. *In the Spirit of Crazy Horse*. New York: Viking Press, 1983.

Messerschmidt, Jim. *The Trial of Leonard Peltier*. Boston: South End Press, 1983.

"The FBI Files." Compiled by the Leonard Peltier Defense Committee, Lawrence, Kansas, 1996.

Chapter 3: The Man Who Never Died

"Don't Mourn—Organize; Songs of Labor Songwriter Joe Hill." CD, 60 min., Smithsonian Folkways, 1990.

Foner, Philip S. *The Case of Joe Hill*. New York: International Publishers, 1965.

Jensen, Vernon H. "The Legend of Joe Hill," *Industrial and Labor Relations Review*, Vol. IV (April 1951) 356–66.

Stavis, Barrie. *The Man Who Never Died: A Play About Joe Hill*. New York: Haven Press, 1954.

Stegner, Wallace. *Joe Hill: A Biographical Novel*. Garden City, New York: Doubleday, 1950.

Chapter 4: A Nation's Vengeance

Balsiger, David and Sellier, Charles E. Jr. *The Lincoln Conspiracy*. Los Angeles: Schick Sunn Classic Books, 1977.

Bishop, Jim. *The Day Lincoln Was Shot*. New York: Harper & Row, Perennial Library Edition, 1964.

Donovan, Robert J. *The Assassins*. New York: Popular Library, 1964.

Kunhardt, Dorothy Meserve and Kunhardt, Philip B. Jr. *Twenty Days*. North Hollywood: Newcastle Publishing Co., 1985.

Kunhardt, Philip B. Jr., Kunhardt, Philip B. III, and Kunhardt, Peter W. *Lincoln, An Illustrated Biography*. New York: Alfred A. Knopf, 1992.

Lattimer, Dr. John. *Kennedy & Lincoln, Medical and Ballistic Comparisons of Their Assassinations*. New York: Harcourt Brace Javanovich, 1980.

"The Surratt Family and John Wilkes Booth." Compiled by James O. Hall, the Surratt Society, Clinton, Maryland, 1993.

Chapter 5: Incident at West Point

Marszalek, John F. *Court-martial: The Army vs. Johnson Whittaker*. New York: Charles Scribner's, 1972.

Marszalek, John F. "A Black Cadet at West Point," *American Heritage* (August 1971), 31–37, 104–106.

"Righting a Historical Wrong," *Ebony* (October 1995), 88–90, 144.

Index

A

Abu-Jamal, Mumia, vii–viii
Alexander, Charles, 122,
    123–124
American Federation of La-
    bor (AFL), 61
American Indian Movement
    (AIM), 34, 42–46. *See also*
    Peltier, Leonard
Arnold, Samuel, 91, 103
Arthur, Chester Alan, 134
Atzerodt, George, 88, 90, 95,
    96–97, 98, 103, 104, 109,
    110

B

Banks, Dennis, 43
Barthel, Joan, 16, 18, 24

Beligni, Jean, 6
Benson, Paul, 47, 48
Booth, John Wilkes, 85, 86
    assassination conspiracy
        of, 93, 94–95, 96–97, 99
    Confederacy and,
        100–101
    kidnap conspiracy and,
        90–91, 92
    Surratt, John, Jr., and,
        87–88
Booth, Junius Brutus, 101
Bornemann, Charles, 22
Bornemann, Jessica, 22
Bureau of Indian Affairs
    (BIA), 43, 44
Burnett, George, 121, 128
Butler, Dino, 36, 37, 46, 48

C

Chamberlain, Daniel H., 132

Chesnut, Mary, 116

Circumstantial evidence, Hill trial, 72

Civil War (U.S.)
end of, 93
Surratt and, 87

Clarvoe, John A. W., 98, 99, 100

Clinton, William J., 52, *137*, 138

Clyburn, James, 137

Coffin, William H., 124

Cohen, Simon, 27

Cohn, Roger, 22, 23

Coler, Jack, 33–36, 46

Connery, Donald, 19–20

Conway, Jim, 21, 22

Cook, William, vii

Criminal justice systems, errors by, vii–ix

D

Daly, T. F. Gilroy, 20, 21, 22, 24, 27

Davis, Benjamin O., 138

Davis, Jefferson, 100

Death penalty, Abu-Jamal and, viii

Doster, William E., 105

E

Eagle, Jimmy, 33, 36, 37

Ekengren, W. A. F., 75, 76

Eselius family, 64, 67

F

Faulkner, Daniel, vii

Fay, John, 82

Federal Bureau of Investigation (FBI)
American Indian Movement and, 43, 44
intimidation by, 47, 48–49
Peltier case and, 31, 35–36, 46–47, 50, 52–53

Florence, Thomas B., 105

Ford, Henry, 135

Ford, John T., 101

Fort Lesley J. McNair, 83, *84*, 85, 104

G

Gardiner, Asa Bird, 133

Gibbons, Barbara, 1, *2*, 23, 29
murder of, 3–4, 7–8
personality of, 6

Grant, U. S., 93

Greener, Richard, 116, 117, 131

H

Hahn, E. E., 74

Hayes, Alfred, 80

Hayes, Rutherford B., 131

Heaney, Gerald W., 49–50

Helpern, Milton, 23, 24, 26

144

Herold, David, 88, 95, 97, 98, *99*, 102–103, 107, 110
Hill, Joe, 56–82, *58*
  arrest of, 67
  birth of, 59
  career of, 60–61
  childhood of, 59–60
  described, 56
  execution of, 78–79
  funeral of, *79*, 79–80
  incident at Salt Lake City, 65–67
  IWW and, 56–57, 62–64
  martyrdom of, 59, 81–82
  media and, 68–69, 77
  sentencing of, 73
  supporters of, *58*, 74–76
  trial of, 57, 69–73
Hillstrom, Joseph, 71
Hodgson, Frederick, 121
Hoge, S. L., 116, 117
Hollings, Ernest F., 136
Hood, John, 125

I

Industrial Workers of the World (IWW), Hill, Joe, 56–57, 62–64, 71, 74, 80. *See also* Hill, Joe
Inouye, Daniel, 49

J

James, Chappie, 138
Johnson, Andrew, 95, 97, 100, 110
Johnson, Reverdy, 106

Jumping Bull, Cecilia, 34, 46
Jumping Bull, Harry, 34, 46

K

Kelly, Timothy, 11
Kennedy, John F., 112
King, Preston, 110
Knauss, Jennifer, 85
Knauss, Walter, 85
Knight, John G. D., 127, 130

L

Lane, James, 110
Lapointe, Richard, 30
Lazelle, Henry M., 122, 123, 124, 125
Leavenworth Federal Penitentiary (Kansas), *53*, 54
Lee, Robert E., 93
Lie-detector tests, Reilly, Peter, 10–11, 29
Lincoln, Abraham, 94
  assassination of, 85, 92, *98*, 99
  kidnap conspiracy against, 87–88, 90–92
Lincoln, Robert Todd, 134
Lippencott, Henry, 124
Lloyd, John, 86, 92, 94, 96, 97, 101, 107, 108, 109

M

MacNeil, Judy, 21–22
Madow, Geoff, 1, 2, 6, 7, 9, 16

Madow, Marion, 3, 4, *5*, 6, 16, 25
Madow, Mickey, 3, 6, 16
Marszalek, John, 136
Matthiessen, Peter, 36, 38, 49
McCafferty, Bruce, 7, 21
McGovern, George, 42
McHugh, Frank, 66
Means, Russell, 43
Miller, Arthur, 18, 20, 24, *28*, 30
Morrison, Arling, 65, 68
Morrison, John, 65, 66, 68
Morrison, Merlin, 65, 69, 70
Mudd, Samuel A., 103

N

Native Americans. *See* Peltier, Leonard
Nichols, Mike, 19
Nixon, Richard, 42
Nothey, John, 93, 94

O

O'Laughlin, Michael, 91, 103, 110
Olsen, Betty Eselius, 64, 67, 70
Osborne, David, 83
Oswald, Lee Harvey, 112

P

Paine, Lewis, 88, 91, 92, 95, 96, 97, 101, 102, 104, 110
Peltier, Betty Ann, 38

Peltier, Leonard, 31–55, *32*
American Indian Movement and, 42–43
attitude of, 32, 55
birth of, 37
career of, 41–42
childhood of, 37–41
defense of, 47–48, 49, *51*, 52, 54
extradition of, 46
imprisonment of, 31
incident at Pine Ridge, 34–36
sentencing of, 47
trial of, 37, 48–49, 50
Pequette, Cecil Whittaker, *137*, 138
Phar, Katie, 60
Pine Ridge Indian Reservation, described, 33. *See also* Peltier, Leonard
Piper, Alexander, 121, 122, 123
Politics
American Indian Movement (AIM), 42–43
Peltier case and, 52
Poor Bear, Myrtle, 46, 48–49
Porter, George Loring, 104
Powell, Colin, 138
Powell, Lewis, 88
Pumphrey, James, 101

R

Red Dog, Greg, *51*
Redford, Robert, 49

Reilly, Peter, 5, *19*, *28*
  appeal of, 19–20
  arrest of, 4, 15
  confession of, 14–15
  detective work for, 20–25
  freeing of, 27–29
  mother's murder and,
    1–4, 7–8
  personality of, 6
  psychiatric examination
    of, 24
  questioning of, 10–14
  sentencing of, 18
  statement of, 8–9
  trial of
    first, 15–18
    second, 25–27
Reno, Janet, 49
Ritchie, M. L., 72, 73, 74
Robeson, Paul, 81
Robideau, Bob, 36, 37, 41,
  46, 48
Robinson, Earl, 80
Ryan, Philip, 130

S

Santore, Dennis, 26, 27
Schofield, John M., 119,
  123, 124, 125, 126, 127
Sears, Clinton, 127,
  128–129, 130, 131
Seeger, Pete, 81, 82
Seeley, Phoebe, 70
Seward, William H., 95, 96,
  97
Shay, James, 8, 10, 11–14, 27

Sherman, William T., 125,
  136
Simpson, Louis, 118
Simpson, O. J., 112
Sitting Bull, 44
Smith, James Webster, 117
Sochocki, John, 3, 9, 21–22
Spangler, Edward (Ned),
  103, 110
Speziale, John A., 26
Spiegel, Herbert, 24, 26
Stanton, Edwin M.,
  100–101, 102, 105, 107
Stavis, Barrie, 81
Stuntz, Joseph Killsright,
  36
Styron, William, 19
Supreme Court (U.S.), cir-
  cumstantial evidence
  and, 72
Surratt, Anna, 86, 100, 110
Surratt, Isaac, 86
Surratt, John, 86, 87
Surratt, John, Jr., 86
  arrest of, 112–113
  Booth and, 87, 91
  conspiracy and, 92, 98
  reward for, *99*
Surratt, Mary, 83–113, *89*
  Booth and, 90, 95–96, 97
  conviction of, 84–85
  execution of, 110, *111*,
    111–112
  life of, 86–87
  suspicions of, 101
  trial of, 96, 102, 103–110

U

U.S. Military Academy,
  Whittaker, Johnson Ches-
  nut and, 114–138. *See
  also* Whittaker, Johnson
  Chesnut
Utah State Prison, 77

W

Wallace, Mike, 24–25
Weichmann, Louis J., 87,
  90, 94, 95, 96, 98, 99, 100,
  107, 108
Wester, Moses, 117
West Point, Whittaker,
  Johnson Chesnut and,
  114–138. *See also* Whittaker, Johnson Chesnut
Whittaker, John, 134
Whittaker, Johnson Ches-
  nut, 114–138, *115*, *135*
  accusation against,
    125–126

awarded commission,
  136, *137*, 137–138
birth of, 114
career of, 134–135
court-martial of, 132–134
court of inquiry, 126–131
death of, 135–136
incident at West Point,
  119–125
life of, 116
nominated to West Point,
  116, 117
religion and, 117–118
support for, 131–132
West Point and, 114–116
Whittaker, Miller, 134
Williams, Ellen, 53
Williams, Ron, 33–36, 46, 53
Williams, Tennessee, 20
Wilson, Dick, 44, 46
Wilson, Woodrow, 74, 76
Wood, William P., 105
Wounded Knee, 44–45